Edward B. (Edward Bond) Foote

**The Radical Remedy in Social Science**

Or, Borning Better Babies through Regulating Reproduction by....

Edward B. (Edward Bond) Foote

**The Radical Remedy in Social Science**
*Or, Borning Better Babies through Regulating Reproduction by....*

ISBN/EAN: 9783337211349

Printed in Europe, USA, Canada, Australia, Japan

Cover: Foto ©Suzi / pixelio.de

More available books at **www.hansebooks.com**

# THE

# Radical Remedy

IN

# SOCIAL SCIENCE;

OR,

# *BORNING BETTER BABIES*

THROUGH

## Regulating Reproduction

BY

## CONTROLLING CONCEPTION.

— — —

*AN EARNEST ESSAY ON PRESSING PROBLEMS,*

BY

*E. B. FOOTE, Jr., M. D.*

———

**Price, 25 Cents.**

NEW-YORK :

MURRAY HILL PUBLISHING COMPANY,

NO. 129 EAST TWENTY-EIGHTH ST.

# PREFATORY NOTE.

This essay is dedicated to serious, thoughtful students of social affairs; to all interested in reforms suggested for the benefit and improvement of humanity; but more especially to "meliorists," those who believe that man can, "by taking thought," do something to better his individual and social state. I make no claim to originality or novelty, and am aware of handling, rather boldly, a subject which many others have but timidly touched upon. Firmly convinced that the argument is right and that it ought to be made, I regard it as timely and necessary, though perhaps for me impolitic. I ask for it earnest consideration and all sorts of criticism, and freely invite all persons, whether thinking well or ill of it, to send me their opinions. I may not need encouragement from those who agree with me, though it would be acceptable, but desire correction from those who disagree. With the hope of ascertaining the average opinion, a large number of copies will be sent to editors, clergymen, physicians, teachers, officers of charitable institutions and members of social science clubs, classes and associations. All are invited to endorse or abuse this work, as they please. I shall be glad to receive expressions of opinion signed or unsigned, and all letters sent marked "confidential" will be held in confidence.

E. B. FOOTE, JR.,

120 Lexington Avenue, N. Y.

April, 1886.

# PROEM.

## CONSENSUS OF THE COMPETENT.

---

" Miserable it is
To be to others cause of misery,
Our own begotten, and of our loins to bring
Into this cursed world a woeful race,
\*    \*    \*    \*    \*; in thy power
It lies, yet ere conception to prevent
The race unblessed, to being yet unbegot."
*Milton's Paradise Lost*, book x.

---

" To a rational being, the prudential check to population ought to be considered as equally natural with the check from poverty and premature mortality."—*Malthus*, 1806.

" Little improvement can be expected in morality until the production of large families is regarded in the same light as drunkenness or any other physical excess."—*John Stuart Mill*, 1872.

" Surely it is better to have thirty-five millions of human beings leading useful and intelligent lives, rather than forty millions struggling painfully for a bare subsistence."—*Lord Derby*, 1879.

"The main cause of distress among the unemployed is the fecundity of the unfit, and this fecundity is as much under the control of a free citizen as the purchase of a weekly dispatch. If this be so, and I am at least satisfied of my facts, surely the time has come when men and women, whose highest wish in life is the welfare of their fellow citizens, may discuss the subject without incurring the hostility of the unco quid."—*A. White, Letter to Weekly Dispatch*, 1885.

"There is no exception to the rule that every organic being naturally increases at so high a rate that, if not destroyed, the earth would soon be covered with the progeny of a single pair. Even the slow breeding man has doubled in twenty-five years, and, at this rate, in a few thousand years, there would literally not be standing room for his progeny."—*Charles Darwin*.

" Artificial selection, now a settled principle in biology, must be applicable in its length and breadth to the human race.   \*   \*   \*
If the opinion could prevail among all classes that the human race could be rapidly improved, both physically and mentally, by the intelligent selection of those who are to keep up the population, much of the difficulty would remove itself. If there is one social phenomenon which human *ingenuity* ought to bring completely under the control of the will, it is the phenomenon of procreation. Just as every one is his own judge of how much he shall eat and

drink, of what commodities he wants to make life enjoyable, so every one should be his own judge of how large a family he desires, and should have power in the same degree to leave off when the requisite number is reached. What society needs is restriction of population, especially among the classes and at the points where it now increases most rapidly."—*From Dynamic Sociology by Lester F. Ward ; Vol. II., Page 463 to 466.*

"To the patient and conscientious observer of social facts, the population question transcends all others, until it is solved all philanthropic movements, reforms and the like, are wont to deepen the very ills they were meant to remove ; or, at most, they end in transferring penalties and burdens from the shoulders of those who have incurred them to their less guilty neighbors. Sanitary reform, education, temperance, in proportion, as they become general, merely intensify the struggle for existence, or, in other words, the internecine war between man and man."—*From the Journal of Science, England.*

"Every one has a right to live. We will suppose this granted. But no one has a right to bring children into life to be supported by other people. Whoever means to stand upon the first of these rights must renounce all pretension to the last. If a man cannot support even himself unless others help him, those others are entitled to say that they do not also undertake the support of any offspring which it is physically possible for him to summon into the world. It would be possible for the State to guarantee employment at ample wages to all that are born. But if it does this, it is bound in self-protection, and for the sake of every purpose for which government exists, to provide that no person shall be born without its consent. Poverty, like most social evils, exists because men follow their brute instincts without due consideration."—*John Stuart Mill in "Political Economy," Chapters XII. and XIII.*

"If men's sympathies are left to work out naturally without legal instrumentality, I hold that the general result will be that the inferior will be sufficiently helped to moderate and alleviate their miseries, but will not be sufficiently helped to enable them to multiply ; and that so the benefit will be achieved without the evil."—*Herbert Spencer in a Letter to M. charmes, the Reviewer of the Work by Spencer—"The Man vs. The State."*

"To refuse marriage to men altogether, or to require them to postpone it indefinitely after the maturity of their judgment has justified their choice, is to inflict an injury on the whole community by encouraging special forms of evil, perhaps even calling them into existence. At present, however, no one thinks of lifting a finger to assist his neighbor in the matter, and as long as such perfect indifference prevails, and an impenetrable veil of mystery is drawn over the whole subject, every man's secret will perish with him, and the advance of the human race in this all-important department of knowledge will, for want of the power of transmission, be no more rapid than that of the brutes."—*Mr. Montagu Cookson, Fortnightly Review, October, 1872.*

# THE RADICAL REMEDY

IN

# SOCIAL   SCIENCE.

SOCIAL SCIENCE or sociology covers the broad field of human interests, the history of man as a social animal, the facts and laws relating to the development of mankind and the organization of tribes and nations. Social Science aims to discover man's place in nature, and the means of improving his condition. Its discussions necessarily lead out in all directions and involve the consideration of a great variety of social science problems appertaining to forms of government, means of subsistence, influences controlling health and disease, the relations of men and women, etc., etc. These problems reaching back as they do to the fundamental principles affecting man's existence, have not materially changed since man became a reasoning animal, and began to study his relations to the outside world and to other men. It required no great scientific acumen for the first settlers on the earth to discover that life is not an unmixed blessing, and that man was not absolved from the struggle for existence, which struggle required him to cope with evils that were regarded as necessary, natural or inevitable, but many of which have been shown to be merely incidental to a state of ignorance of nature's facts and forces. In the infancy of mankind, when the immature mind awakened to a consciousness of dangers on every hand and innumerable evils which

it could trace to no better source than Pandora's box or
Eve's transgression, the endeavor to escape these evils
by propitiation of the gods was a matter of course,
while at the same time there was a humble submission
to the superstition that man could not successfully contend with the forces of nature.

### Progress Under Scientific Methods.

About three hundred years ago the era of science
dawned, and with it came the scientific method of
thought in the elucidation of all problems that had mys-
tified and perplexed mankind. Its first brilliant
achievements were in astronomy, physics and chemistry, but gradually enlarging its operations it has practically dominated in biology, culminating in the grand
doctrine of evolution; and now, undaunted, it marches
on with confidence into those domains of knowledge
which are most intimately associated with human interests—the domain of Social Science. Scientific methods
have not only accomplished great results in mathemat-
ics, astronomy, physics and chemistry, but also in the
practical arts, revolutionizing commerce, industry and
governments, creating institutions of learning, remod-
eling dwellings and cities, improving the methods of
living with an increase of home comforts. In short, *the
scientific method is now the art of civilization*, and all efforts
for the perfection of civilization in order to be successful must be in accordance with the scientific method.

It is therefore important to have a thorough understanding of the scientific method, the essence of
which in the domain of applied social science is to

### "Learn What is True in Order to Do What is Right,"

a maxim of Descarte's, and which is, as I take it, the essence of Herbert Spencer's summing up of the utility
of all philosophy in his book entitled, "The Data of

Ethics." Science seeks the true for its own sake, and having found it, takes it unto itself without fear of consequences. Science is argus-eyed, searches in all directions for truth, accepts it from any and every source, and assimilates everything which will bear investigation. True social science studies all sorts and conditions of men, their manners and customs, virtues and vices, and reports them impartially, without fear or favor, without prejudice or disgust. It regards with interest all problems relating to the improvement and welfare of mankind, and treats each according to its importance. The thorough social scientist will not hesitate to enter upon the study of any social evil because it is tabooed by amateur philanthropists, and if there be anything that has been neglected by others who fear to soil their dainty hands with it, he will pursue the noisome evil to its source, drag it from its hidden retreat and expose it to the disinfecting sunlight of publicity. He will be apt to discover in the forbidding fields and low-lying grounds the foul brooding places of

### Fatal Physical, Moral and Social Epidemics.

If he be a practical man and a consistent advocate of the scientific method in all things, he will apply it to the solution of these social science problems in an effective way which will strike deep down at the root of all evil. In looking about for remedies for social science evils he will be broad and liberal-minded, and will no more expect to find a universal panacea than he would to discover the balm of perpetual youth. But neither would he, in his search for remedies, permit himself to be turned aside from the consideration of any remedy which could receive the endorsement of science and give fair promise of usefulness, merely because it could not find favor in the eyes of antiquarians. He will be frightened away by no scarecrow of ancient superstition set up in the path of progress. Nor will he be deterred from favoring a remedy because someone raises the cry that it is "unnatural"—meaning that it is not in accord with what Nature intended, or that it will interfere with Nature's processes and results. From one point of view all our material progress has been due to thwarting Nature—evading Nature's decrees - but the scientist really takes advantage of one natural law to protect himself against another, manipulates natural forces within his control so as to make them protect him against those beyond his control.

### Science Applied to Nature's Forces.

The ancient's first impertinence in the eyes of the gods was the stealing of the fire of Heaven and putting it to his own use, which man has done in innumerable ways, until he now makes steam do the greater part of the labor of the world—the more civilized world. The modern man has been vastly more audacious in stealing the fire of Heaven, for since the example of our great philosopher, Benjamin Franklin, who went fishing for chained-lightning and caught it, the inventions of men have saddled this swift steed and tamed him for our use. Other modern discoveries now recognized to be of great value have given us wonderful control over pain, one of the oldest and most natural evils, but *to relieve pain is to stifle the voice of Nature;* and when anæsthetics were proposed for the relief of the pains of childbirth it was seriously opposed by those who quoted the ancient scriptural injunction, which reads: "In sorrow thou shalt bring forth children." This opposition was of no avail; anæsthesia was the child of science, and in the face of all opposition has become a universal remedy for human pain.

All sanitary remedies are opposed to what may be called natural evils; but right here is the great difference

between the old and the new thought—the old idea
being that certain evils were natural or inevitable, to be
avoided only by petitions, charms, incantations and
immolations, having no knowledge or thought of man's
own ability to discover and apply natural remedies for
natural evils, while this is the very essence of the new
thought of the scientific era.

### Social Evils—Ancient and Modern.

In scanning the budget of social evils which perplex
the humanitarian of our time, it is easy to see that most
of them are of very ancient origin.   They can be traced
back as far as history reaches; many can be recognized
as part of that very lot that escaped from Pandora's box.
They are evidently relics of barbarism, which the advance of civilization has not been able to leave behind.
Some of them seem to have been a little diminished and
others even intensified by the change towards civilization, while a few are entirely of modern origin—new
inventions resulting from that dangerous thing, a little
knowledge;  or maybe, merely protean  evils in new
forms.

It may be interesting to make a list of the social evils
now existing in so-called civilized communities. But in
so doing, we must remember that they are all as intimately related as the members of one family; that they
act and re-act upon one another, each one helping more
or less to increase the rest; and furthermore, it is important to remember that while some are mostly social
evils and others more particularly affect the individual,
they are all so far-reaching in their consequences and so
ramified in their branches that it would be impossible
to draw any definite line of that kind between them.
Some may be regarded as being mainly unhealthful or
unsanitary evils, while others remind us forcibly of
their cost to society, their wastefulness and tax upon

the body-politic.   While the latter may be pre-eminently
checks upon national prosperity, all but what I shall
call the radical evils are what Malthus called positive
checks to population.   For he says, "The positive
checks are extremely numerous and include every cause,
whether arising from vice or misery, which in any degree contributes to shortening the duration of life."
The positive checks may be classified as regular or
incidental, but not by hard and fast lines.   Probably
the most interesting and useful study of social evils is
for the purpose of discovering the *radical evils*, and if
we were to picture them as a great upas tree, it would
be in order to write ignorance upon the roots, reckless
propagation on the trunk leading to one great branch,
called over-population, and to another called evil hereditary tendencies, while in the entangled branches would
be found the luxuriant crop of individual and social
evils.   But for lack of the picture we will arrange them
as follows:

Radical Evils.

    Ignorance,
    Reckless  Propagation,
    Evil Hereditary Influences,
    Over-Population.

Positive Population Checks (Vice and Miseries).

Regular Checks.

    Famines,
    Plagues,
    Wars,
    Abortion,
    Infanticide,
    Baby-farming,
    Disease,
    Deformities—Blindness, Deafness,
    Death—Premature.

Incidental Checks.

    Pauperism,
    Drunkenness,
    Crime,
    Imbecility,
    Idiocy,
    Insanity,
    Overcrowding, Tenements, etc.,
    Uncleanliness,
    Squalor,
    Immorality,
    Prostitution,
    Contagious Diseases.

## Social Science Problems.

Various Social Science problems arise from the consideration of these evils as factors, and involve the discussion of questions relating to monopoly of power, land and money; the rights of men, women and children; the relation of capital, labor and business; the regulation of commerce, transportation and trade; the conditions affecting population, subsistence and immigration. So, reforms of various kinds are being constantly brought for the relief of social evils and the amelioration of human suffering. Many useful reforms have naturally attended our progress toward civilization, causing manifest improvement in the diminution of famines, plagues and wars; but in whatever direction improvement is noticed, it is easy to show that it has been due to the advance in knowledge and inventions—to following out scientific methods in certain directions where it has been practicable so to do.

Our grade of civilization, happiness, comforts and freedom from evils of various kinds, can be judged somewhat by the study of mortality tables—the determination on the average length of life. In 1877 the following appeared in the Sanitarian:

Medical Science, in its preventive aspect, especially, shows a steady advance in its ability to discover, prevent and check diseases, which in the past ages devastated large communities. In London, for instance, in two centuries the mortality was 50 per 1,000, and the average duration of life only twenty years. The death-rate 1661-79, 80; 1716-55, 35.5; 1846-55, 24.9; 1871, about as at present, 22.6, and the mean duration of life is now forty-two years. The subject of public hygiene has received great attention of recent years, and its difficulties are being steadily overcome. Men, unquestionably, live longer now than their ancestors did, and have far better average health, and that our descendants will gain on us in these respects there is but little reason to doubt.

### "The Human Race Threatened."

Whether our descendants shall gain on us or not, and in what proportion, must depend upon whether we are

wise in our day and generation, and to what extent we
are ready to sense our situation, assimilate new ideas
and to act upon the dictates of the scientific method.
Instead of spending time in mutual congratulations on
the improvements which have been effected in three
centuries past, we may more profitably consider our
present situation and what remains to be done, and what
can reasonably be done by us. Nothing mundane is in
a state of *statu-quo*. The earth keeps moving, and with
it all its inhabitants; and nations, like men, are moving
either forward or backward, improving or degenerating.
There are tides in the affairs of men—a movement of
ebb and flow—and there may be advance in one locality
while there is retrogression in another, and in any one
community there may be advance in some affairs and
retrogression in others at the same time. So, even in
one State only at any given time, it is an extremely difficult and complicated problem to discover the general
social status and tendency. In a book, called "Deter-
ioration and Race Education" (Lee & Shepard, 1878) by
Mr. Samuel Royce, he "comes to the conclusion that
the human race is threatened with degenerating tendencies." In support of this conclusion he cites a large
number of statistics which certainly show a condition of
things serious enough to excite alarm; but they are
gathered from many countries at varying periods of
time, and complicate rather than assist a solution of the
problem of the general tendency of the human race,
whether for better or worse. But he truly remarks that
practical reforms lag far behind good suggestions for
reform—"We have applied science to almost everything
and have made it pay, save to humanity itself."

The experts in social science are yet to be born, but
the panaceas for the ills of humanity are already numerous and the inventors with a patent millennial social

order or a perfect economic system, are like the poor, "always with you." Each leads his hobby confidentially to the scratch, prepared to demonstrate its good points and its ability to run down the hounds of social vice and misery, and as of old it was said "all ways lead to Rome," so now we are offered

### Many Straight Roads to the Millennium.

A man with prohibition on the brain will trace everything to alcoholism and its long train of evil consequences. The labor reformer will see our way out of them all through some readjustment of social relations for the abolition of poverty and the incentives to crime. The tenement-house reformer will appeal for legislation to do away with overcrowded tenements, and will be able to cite instances of great diminution in vice and crime where his recommendations have been carried out. The State socialist will request that all men, women and children not capable of providing for themselves shall become the wards of the State, and become self-supporting in educational and industrial institutions; and he will perhaps go so far as to lay out a full programme of parallel methods by which social evils shall be rapidly cured. The "societies for the suppression of" vice, crime and cruelties have each in their way discovered how to repress these several evils, and when they shall have carried out their scheme to their satisfaction and its logical conclusion, the whole population will be provided for in penal institutions, asylums and reformatories, and the last man will have crept in and turned the key after him. The ultra-anarchist will cry, "Hands off, a fair field and no favor; let natural selection and the survival of the fittest have full swing, and hurrah for the best man." Inasmuch as I have my own radical remedy for social evils, no time will be given to any consideration or comparison of the merits of other plans.

## Scientific Education the Broad Basis of all Reforms.

First, let me call to my aid the social science expert as far as he has been developed, and ask him to endorse my arrangement of social evils, or more especially the position assigned to ignorance at the head of the column as the radical evil. It requires no argument to precede the statement that education is the basis of all scientific reforms, and science calls for a thorough, liberal and systematic education in the place of the ordinary schooling and exclusive literary culture which has been heretofore thought to constitute a good education. Science demands physical, physiological, moral, industrial and intellectual education, recognizing the importance of every branch, but would, perhaps, give preference to those that are most immediately necessary to the development of the functions and faculties of man in order to render him a healthful, happy and long-lived animal, and a worthy member of society. Essays and books on educational reform demonstrate the necessity for revising educational methods, and are sufficiently numerous. Indeed, the preaching is far ahead of the practice. It is easy to start out in any direction and show how better educational methods would vastly improve the condition of things. Physical education, the proper exercise and training of the muscles and special senses, would, through improving health and strength, lesson the evils resulting from disease, deformity and enervation. Industrial education would confer dexterity of hand and fertility of thought, diminish thriftlessness, incompetency and pauperism, and do much toward making everyone self-supporting. Physiological, hygienic and sanitary education will work against personal vice and public nuisances. Moral education, when based, as to be effective it must be, upon the scientific data of ethics, will also be a powerful factor in the repression of social

evils for we all detect a hopeful amount of well-meaning
—a desire to do right if one could only know what is
true.   A high intellectual education of the true scientific
order, involving a complete philosophy of life and
founded upon a thorough knowledge of the sciences,
may some time provide us with the new catechism and
a means of knowing what is right under all circumstances, which is the object of the synthetic philosophy
of Herbert Spencer, as stated in the preface to the
"Data of Ethics," where he defines the ultimate purpose of his life's work to be "that of finding for the
principles of right and wrong in conduct at large, a
scientific basis."

### Scotch Evils at Their Source.

From previous considerations we may conclude that
ignorance is the root of all evil, and education the radical remedy; but a further analysis of the modus operandi of ignorance as a source of evil will better enable
us to determine in what especial direction education is
most needed, in order to limit evils arising from ignorance.   It is really but a short step to the discovery of
the way in which this satan —ignorance, and all his
angels are perpetuated.   Ignorance leaves man open
to the full play of his passional impulses, and there
results an excessive, reckless, hap-hazard propagation of
the race, in which there is a sort of go-as-you-please contest between the natural virtues and vices of man, none
of the contestants appearing to have any advantage over
the others until scientific education stepped in as backer
of his better qualities, and under such training the virtues certainly ought to win; for scientific education
gives man a cue by which to scotch evils at their source
   that is, intelligent restriction of propagation or prudential checks.

This is a valuable cue or suggestion, but one requiring good judgment for its safe application, lest in handicapping the vices we crowd out virtues as well; and, furthermore, a too radical application of this remedy would blot out mankind altogether. "Genius to madness is oft close allied," and sometimes those who are regarded by the world at large as most mad, are, in fact, the greatest geniuses. John Stewart Mill has said that we ought not to try to reduce the world to one dead level of equality by suppressing the eccentricities, the peculiar people, the odd geniuses, who are often, in fact, the only people of original thought. Many of us would be utterly opposed to any legislation forbidding so-called cranks from marrying, not so much from personal motives either, as from a knowledge that the world would have no advanced ideas, and hence, no progress without a fair proportion of this element. Virtues and vices have their bonds of affinity; an exaggerated virtue becomes a vice as too much of a good thing is good for nothing; and if the radical remedy were given too severe a logical application no man having a physical or moral vice or imperfection would reproduce his kind, and the race would stop short, like grandfather's clock never to go again—for we are none of us perfect—"no, not one."

## The Radical Remedy Stated.

We shall find that in whatever direction we may start out to make a study of social evils, we shall be sure to trace the thread of our investigation to the one great all-pervading factor of ignorance operating through reckless propagation to produce over-population and evil hereditary influences, and a full appreciation of this fact leads us to the conclusion that we must find the remedy in that line of study and education which shall enable and induce all people to regulate reproduction. We want :—

A sufficient education in the science of private and public hygiene and morals, and especially in the direction of sex, reproduction and heredity, which shall be so general that every man and woman at the age of puberty shall know enough, and be religiously inclined to guard against crippling himself or herself, the family or society, by indulging in vice of any kind, and particularly that of reckless propagation.

This is the *radical remedy*, a thorough one, and Utopian enough for the most devout optimist. Even though it be an electric beacon in whose bright light we may not hope to bask, as 'neath the noonday sun, yet for us its dim rays already show the way to brighter days, and point out the line of progress we should pursue. The first steps to be taken in this direction will be considered in the following chapters.

# CHAPTER II.

## The Law of Excess or Waste Operating in Positive Population Checks.

THE Malthusian statement of the law of population has received its most fierce criticism from Henry George in "Progress and Poverty," and doubtless there is much truth in his argument that where population appears to be excessive, with resulting vice and misery, such evils might readily be overcome by a more equable distribution of products, through more just social arrangements. It is nevertheless true that if men were living under social arrangements which should supply the wants of everyone, and render all perfectly comfortable, population would increase more rapidly than it has ever been known to do, and the day of scarcity would inevitably and in fact very rapidly approach.

Mr. Moncure D. Conway, the well-known London correspondent of the Cincinnati Commercial, wrote not long ago : "The question of increase of population in this country is a terrible one, an urgent one. The struggle for existence has become a civil war. The Malthusian question is up, and nothing can put it down."

Other students of English and European affairs declare that Malthusianism is not the imminent question, that present difficulties may be overcome and threatened dangers averted by devising methods for the more equable distribution of the world's products. For instance, M. Elisee Reclus, the eminent author of historical and geographical works, in the Contemporary Review, writes:

Whatever may be the value of Malthus' forecast as to the distant future, it is an actual incontestable fact that in civilized countries of Europe and America the sum total of provisions produced, or received in exchange for manufactures, is more than enough for the sustenance of the people. Even in times of partial dearth the granaries and warehouses have but to open their doors that everyone may have a sufficient share. Notwithstanding waste and prodigality, despite the enormous losses arising from moving about and handling in warehouses and shops, there is always enough to feed generously all the world.

### Malthusianism a Family Matter.

In a New York Tribune editorial on the revival of Malthusianism in Germany in the year 1882, this sentence occurred: "Increase of population is only one of the many factors entering into the complex problems of national well-being," but it is also one of the factors entering into the complex problems of family life, and it is by no means as difficult in a family as in a nation or state to discover when "there is an increase in the number of mouths over the powers of the working hands to feed them," as Henry George puts it. However unimportant the Malthusian law may be in problems affecting nations, there is no dodging the fact that in every separate family the question of the increase of members is likely to become a very important matter, one in which every member of the family must be vitally interested, whether he knows it or not: for when the income is pretty definitely limited it is certain that every newcomer will shorten the rations of his predecessors, and probably be himself limited to an allowance which would really not be sufficient for his needs. When one sees—as I have, and as many a dispensary physician

has—a child born into a family where there are already
four small children, almost no furniture and actually no
food in the house, and no clothing for the new-comer
except a thin blanket, and no prospect of a better state
of affairs until the mother shall have recovered sufficient
strength to take in washing, there we have, beyond a
doubt, an instance of population pressing too closely on
sustenance. When we see families in factory towns, as
any one may, if the reports of the Massachusetts and
New Jersey labor bureaus are true, in which the earnings of the father are insufficient to support the family,
where children from five to twelve years of age supply
perhaps a fourth of the family earnings, necessitating
their employment during twelve hours a day in occupations that stunt their growth, pave the way for early
demise and render any systematic education impossible, there we have a chance to observe some of the evil
effects of over-population, *under existing conditions.*
When we read of the fearful crowding of tenements, of
the suffering of children in such quarters from the lack
of space, food and clothing; of their death from suffoca-
tion from overlying, of the prevalence of wasting and
filth diseases, of the high infantile mortality rate; when
we read the daily reports of infanticides, desertions of
babes, the success of baby-farming enterprises, or of the
rapid increase of childrens' deaths in an English town
after the establishment of burial societies which pay a
stated sum on the death of an infant, often a source of
profit to the parents when a child is entered in several
burial clubs—when it is clearly impossible for us to
estimate the full extent of such inhuman crimes, is it
not evident that there are numerous individual instances where no increase of family can occur without
detriment to that family, and probably to society also?
Is not every new-comer under such circumstances an
unwelcome guest whose visit to this world is sure to be

an unmitigated evil, both because of its own sickly and painful life and early death, and because of the demoralization of the family which thus becomes hardened to criminal neglect of its own progeny?   In my experience as a student among the dispensary patients of this city I once met a woman who had had and lost seven children, and who spoke of the loss with as little feeling as Artemus Ward did of his wife's relations.   "The Lord had given them and the Lord had taken them away; blessed be the Lord."   There is too much of this sort of resignation, and far too little appreciation of the responsibilities of parentage.

### Too Frequent Child-Bearing.

When it is announced by the Daily Graphic that the farmers of this country use up on the average two and a half wives each, by the too great strain to which they are subjected in the effort to do a woman's work about a farm-house, in addition to the cares and contingencies of maternity; when we hear a physician who makes a specialty of diseases of women (in the Medical Record), declare that "one of the most marked and important causes of insanity in women was clearly traceable to frequent child-bearing and lactation among the poorer classes, that there was too little in our literature on the subject of mania caused by the exhaustion of the nervous system by child-bearing and nursing;" when we discover in reports of insane asylums that a large proportion of the inmates are farmers' wives, we may put these facts together and discover that reckless propagation (frequent child-bearing) is largely responsible for the breaking down of women in body and mind, and it becomes a pretty safe conclusion that it would be wise to conserve the health and sanity of the mothers of the land by affording them a means of protection against excessive and untimely maternity.

Dr. Stearns, in an annual report of the Hartford Retreat for the Insane, relates the case of an Englishman,
the father of eight children, whose wife was brought to
the asylum for treatment. The husband innocently
remarked : "Her is a most domestic woman; her is
always doing something for her children; her is always
at work for us all. Her never goes out of the house—
not even to church on Sunday. Her never goes gadding
about the neighbors' houses or talking from one to
another. Her always had the boots blacked in the
morning. Her has been one of the best wives and
mothers, and was always at home."

Every physician who has to do with the diseases common to women is daily compelled to note the fact that
a large number of cases are directly traceable to excessive and ill-timed child-bearing; that from this cause
their nerve-strength is exhausted, rendering them easy
victims to the diseases of debility, and also to death in
the act of labor from no other cause than mere exhaustion—the act calling for more strength than the body
can afford, and death comes as from the shock of an
operation.

### Malthus' Law--The Law of Waste.

Malthusianism as a national question is an interesting
one, involving as it does, a study of the possible rate of
increase of a people living under favorable conditions,
their power to make the earth yield products for their
sustenance, and the possibility, in the course of time, of
a population too great in numbers to be assured a suffi-
ciency of food products. This phase of the question
the writer is content to leave to future generations, hoping that long before it shall have become a live-issue in
America, other more pressing national questions relating
to labor and the distribution of the products of labor
will have been satisfactorily solved, so that it may be

possible for the United States to give practical proof of
how large a population (how many inhabitants to the
acre) this land can comfortably support, as it has already
proved during one hundred years of existence that Malthus' ratio of a population doubling itself every twenty-
five years is possible. It is sufficient for my purpose
here and now to show, as has just been done, how
over-population, or as it is better called under such
circumstances, excessive child-bearing, operates to
the detriment of comfort, the sacrifice of health, over-
work, overcrowding, puny offspring, squalor and pauperism with their attendant vices, crimes and miseries, and necessarily results in a great waste of
health and wealth. While it may be entirely too soon
to raise the cry that there is danger of general famine in
the United States if the population is permitted to go on
increasing during the next hundred years as rapidly as
it has during the first century of the Republic, it is certainly not too soon to call attention to the fact that reckless, hap-hazard, unrestrained, unregulated propagation
is productive of vice, misery and crime; that, in fact,
people who delight to call themselves civilized, permit
themselves to be controlled in the matter of reproduction by the law of waste, prodigality or extravagance,
which prevails among all lower forms of life. Malthus'
"Law of Population," as applied to the human race, is
but one expression of this general Law of Waste or
Excess in generation which is observed throughout
nature, and which, even the disputers of Malthusianism
do not deny. The following excellent statement of this
law is from the Popular Science Monthly :

### Life and Death in Nature.

For some inscrutable reason, which she has as yet given no hint
of revealing, Nature is wondrously wasteful in the matter of generation. She creates a thousand where she intends to make use of
one. Impelled by maternal instinct, the female cod casts millions

of eggs upon the waters, expecting them to return after many days as troops of interesting offspring. Instead, half the embryotic gadi are almost immediately devoured by spawn caters, hundreds of thousands perish in incubation, hundreds of thousands more succumb to the perils attending ichthyic infancy, leaving but a few score to attain to adult usefulness, and pass an honored old age, with the fragrance of a well-spent life in a country grocery.

The oak showers down ten thousand acorns, each capable of producing a tree. Three-fourths of them are straightway diverted from their arboreal intent, through conversion into food by the provident squirrel and the improvident hog. Great numbers rot uselessly upon the ground, and the few hundreds that finally succeed in germinating grow up in a dense thicket, where at last the strongest smothers out all the rest, like an oaken Othello in a harem of quercine Desdemonas.

This is the law of all life, animal as well as vegetable. From the humble hyssop on the wall to the towering cedar of Lebanon—from the meek and lowly amœba, which has no more character or individuality than any other pin point of jelly—to the lordly tyrant, man, the rule is inevitable and invariable. Life is sown broadcast, only to be followed almost immediately by a destruction nearly as sweeping. Nature creates by the million, apparently that she may destroy by the myriad. She gives life one instant, only that she may snatch it away the next. The main difference is that, the higher we ascend, the less lavish the creation, and the less sweeping the destruction. Thus, while probably one fish in a thousand reaches maturity, of every 1,000 children born 604 attain adult age. That is, nature flings aside 999 out of every 1,000 fishes as useless for her purposes, and two out of every five human beings.

### "Slaughter of the Innocents."

It is against the permission of the evil operation of this law of waste of life in the human species that I desire to enter a loud protest. The last sentence of the above quoted article may be a fair general statement of the comparative loss in human beings from birth to maturity, but at times, and in some localities, the loss approaches ninety per cent. in the first year of life, according to the statement of M. Bergeron concerning some parts of France, who also says, "While the mortality among infants is greater in France than among the northern countries of Europe, it is less in Spain,

Prussia, Italy, Austria, Russia or Bavaria. An infant at birth has less probability of living a year than a man eighty years of age." On the other side can be cited the fact that in one of our American communities the Oneida) but one child died during seven years among sixty children born and reared there. In order to know just what the loss of human life amounts to among a certain class or number of people it would be necessary to find out just how many products of conception reached maturity, and how many fell by the wayside; for the loss includes all abortions, whether accidental or designed, as well as deaths resulting from accidents of labor, infantile diseases or diseases of childhood, and were the facts for such a reckoning ascertainable, it might often be found that the loss or waste of human life in the race for maturity approximates close to that of fishes.

This waste of human life, though always as yet inestimable, is always considerable, must to some extent be inevitable, but we must recognize that it is also to a large extent avoidable. In the never-ending struggle for existence among living things the Law of Sacrifice, by which one form of life is made to yield itself up that another, higher or mightier, may live, is as widespread in its operations as the Law of Excess in generation, and the Law of Sacrifice is manifest in its worst phase among men in cannibalism ; but though it requires only a low grade of civilization to rise above this, it seems that we are yet a long way from that grade of civilization which shall as earnestly protest against the needless operation amongst us of the Law of Waste, Excess or Profligacy in propagation. Therefore there is in our great centres of population a "slaughter of the innocents" equal to that of barbaric times, and following the same methods  Dr. Alexander Wilder, a scholarly writer upon medical as well as miscellaneous literary topics, wrote in 1876 :

The Phœnicians, their colonies, and people under their influence, made the immolation of children a religious matter; and the Jews especially, whose prophets declared children to be a blessing from God, nevertheless were like their neighbors in this matter.  Jerusalem was "filled from one end to another with innocent blood;" there being an altar for the purpose on every street.—Jeremiah, xi: 13, and xix: 4-5.  In modern Europe child-killing is practised somewhat differently.  Foundling hospitals exist to take the matter off the hands of the parents, and baby-farming which seems to be a method of killing by inches, finishes up the work.  In this country the practices of the Old World have been learned and imitated with extraordinary facility.  Usually as suggested by Hudibras, our people compound

> " For sins they are inclined to,
> By damning those they have no mind to."

Dr. Thadeus Reamy, of Cincinnati, Professor of Obstetrics in the Ohio Medical College, made the following assertion two years ago: "There are members of the *regular* profession in this city, otherwise of high standing, whose hands are bloody with the guilt of the crime of abortion; and abortion is committed by the wives of respectable citizens, who are taught to do so by their family physicians."  The Academy of Medicine, after appointing a Committee of Inquiry, exculpated Dr. Reamy from any imputation of falsehood or exaggeration; after which he added that he would not confine his assertion to that city, but would include the whole country.  We have seen no attempt to disprove his charges.  It seems, therefore, that abortion is not considered of itself a heinous offence, but is a business in the province of members of the *regular* profession, and does not detract from their "high standing."  Our professed embryo-killers and fœticides are offenders, it would seem, not because they commit crimes, but because not being "otherwise of high standing," they have made a specialty of the business which belongs to the "regular" practitioner.

### Fœticide and Infanticide.

Dr. Wilder's conclusion is abundantly substantiated by the reports of court proceedings in New York city, from which it appears that an accident or misfortune leading to the conviction of a professed abortionist is pretty sure to cause him or her to be sent up for a long term of years, though regular practitioners brought before the courts, as they frequently are, upon the same charge, manage to evade the penalty of the law. The former is apt to be looked upon as a "butcher" lacking the requisite skill in a delicate business self-assumed, and gets the full measure of the law, while the latter, if of sufficient "high standing," or having political influence, is leniently treated, and there is found for him some ready loop-hole of the law or flaw in the evidence. It is with especial readiness that such court proceedings are hushed up if the accident following an abortive operation happens with a married woman, and in the opinion of Dr. H. S. Storer, author of "Why Not," "the act is proportionately much more common in the married than in the unmarried." On the other hand he believes that infanticide is the more common resort when "accidents" happen in unmarried women. The New York Medical Record of July 12, 1884, contained a long editorial on "Infanticide in This City," quoting the statistics of the coroner's records which showed that "during four months and a half the police had picked up in various parts of Manhattan Island, the bodies of forty-five children ranging in age from a few hours to two months." This editorial says "the police apparently regard infanticide as a necessary evil, and make no attempt to discover its perpetrators. The real reason they make no effort to unearth the murderers of children is not the lack of evidence, but the lack of inducement. These poor murdered children never had the right to exist, and if they are made away with no one grieves or pines. The unhappy mother is rid of a burden, the father of a stumbling block and the world of a bastard. The child itself is better off too, is the argument of the practical. All of which may be true; but shame on a social system which makes infanticide possible by teaching that it is a crime for a child to be born! One truth stands out in bold relief, and that is that fœticide and infanticide are looked upon to-day with a feeling akin to indifference."

The Coroner's records cannot be a fair indication of the extent of the evil of infanticide; the ash-barrels, dirt-heaps and vacant lots which provide coroners' cases not being the favorite places of deposit of the evidences of such crimes, for the dark sewers and wide rivers are readier and safer places—graves that seldom yield up their dead—and it is therefore impossible to make any estimate of the loss of life in this way. But we may trust that the evil is rather less common with us than in less "moral" or enlightened countries; and we may, indeed, assume that the "refinements" of our civilization would tend to invite a resort to the less openly brutal practice of fœticide. Dr. Storer says, "Not only is abortion of excessively frequent occurrence; the nefarious practice is yearly extending, as does every vice that custom and habit render familiar." And the author of "A Woman's Thoughts About Women" writes: "Ladies boast to each other of the impunity with which they have aborted as they do of their expenditures, of their dress, of their success in society."

It would, of course, be no more easy to arrive at a correct estimate of the waste of life from fœticide than of that due to infanticide, but every reference to these subjects by moralists and sanitarians is mainly to deplore their frequency and enormity. Of fœticide it must be remembered that the evil is not alone the aborting of embryo life, but also because it is wasteful of the health of women, and because one voluntary act of this kind paves the way for involuntary repetitions. Furthermore, it is unfortunate for children to be born of mothers whose health has been broken down by frequent abortions. No lengthy argument to substantiate these facts is needed here. The facts are to be found in all authoritative works on the subject. It is sufficient for my purpose to call attention to the prevalence of fœticide and infanticide, their wastefulness of human life and health, and especially the fact that (with rare exceptions appertaining to abortion) they are unnecessary and avoidable evils.

### Baby-Farming, Foundling Asylums and Infant Insurance.

IN countries so far advanced as to have laws making infanticide criminal and dangerous, people who are bound not to be burdened with the results of their profligacy and recklessness in reproduction have resource to baby-farming, or consign unwelcome guests to foundling asylums. The business of baby-farming is carried on in such a quiet and private way that we know and hear but little of it excepting as now and then some small institution for the purpose gets into trouble and affords the basis of a sensational newspaper article, but the terrific mortality of infants in foundling asylums is a constant factor in our mortality statistics; not because of any criminal intent or carelessness in such institutions, but because of the inevitable high death-rate among infants brought up "on the bottle," and also because the neglected waifs are largely an ill-begotten lot, and lack vital tenacity.

Still another method of slaughtering the innocents is the gradual freezing out process practised in London, where, according to the statement of a religious weekly paper, "the books of the insurance companies show that the death rate among the infants who are insured is much greater than the death rate for the same ages as published in government reports. These facts strengthen the suspicion into conviction that many infants are deliberately murdered for the sake of the insurance on their lives. The insurance companies which accept

risks on infant lives will insure none but healthy children, and consequently the mortality among them
would naturally be less than among the general average
of children.  Several of the medical and legal papers
are imploring Parliament to devise some remedy for the
growing and horrible evil."  This old and well-grounded
custom of the Old World has not yet been adopted in
America, in spite of the general reputation of its people
for devious modes of money getting; but the existence
of such a scheme of insurance frauds illustrates the
possible depths of moral degradation amongst those
conditions of living which are accompanied by over-
population and all its attendant evils.

When newsboys rush through the streets shouting
loudly,

### "Great Loss of Life."

the interest of the public is quickly aroused, and if a
few hundred lives have been lost in a railroad or steam-
boat accident the people want to know how and why,
and whether any one has been careless.  They propose
to hold somebody responsible, and to prevent, so far as
possible, similar accidents in the future.  But by fœticide, infanticide, over-crowding, famine, filth, drunkenness and disease, there is every day in every large city, a
cruel and terrific loss of life that arouses but little interest, and in the application of remedies, results in
administering brandy, paregoric and vaccination to a
few babes and the sending of a few more for a day or a
week at the seaside, while the majority go "over the
river."

Supposing the human embryo has not been nipped in
the bud, has not died a-borning and finds a fair welcome
at its mother's breast, what are its prospects of reaching
maturity and becoming an acceptable citizen?  Not
temptingly favorable under good conditions, and when

a child is born in a poor, over-crowded family, or a poor, over-populated quarter, its chances of making any score at all in a race of twenty-one years is disheartening to think of; and if such could know in advance the dangers ahead it is supposable that it might not have the pluck to try to run the gauntlet of neglect, starvation, numerous infantile and zymotic diseases, over-laying, bad diet, impure water, sewer gas and even poisoned candy, with the prospect that before it is in its teens it will be put to some fatal factory work and come to a premature end from bad air or over-work. In New York city, during the height of the summer season about one hundred infants succumb daily to the adverse influences into which they were born. Someone has said for them:

"If so soon I was done for,
Then what was I begun for."

The National Reformer (London) reported in 1878 an inquest on the body of a child that was suffocated by being overlaid by its mother, who testified that she, her husband and five children lived in one room, and that seven out of twelve children were already buried. The coroner remarked, "That is the old tale, gentlemen; half the manhood of London sacrificed in consequence of the want of fresh air and proper sanitary arrangements."

### Waste! Waste!! Waste!!!

Whatever view may be taken of the law of population, there is no denying the fact that in keeping population up to its present standard or rate of increase there is immense *waste* of health and life, of women's health and life; immense *waste* of men's industry and capital; immense *waste* of the sources of national prosperity. A Nation's strength is not only in the *number* of its people, but also in their *quality*, and a Nation's prosperity will be in proportion to the health, activity and industry of the industrious classes. Writers on political economy produce statistics to show the average loss of working days to each individual through sickness, and argue that the sum total of time thus lost through illness is economic waste.

"In Massachusetts, during the seven years from 1865 to 1871, 72,700," says Dr. Jarvis, "died in their working period. In the fullness of life and the fullness of health they would have opportunity of laboring for themselves, their families and the public, in all, three million six hundred thousand years. But the total of their labors amounts only to one million six hundred thousand years, leaving a loss of one million nine hundred thousand years by their premature deaths."

A million nine hundred thousand years of labor lost in Massachusetts between 1865 and 1871 by the premature deaths of 72,000 in their working period! "This was an average annual loss of 276,000 years of service! Thus it appears," continues this official document, "that in Massachusetts—one of the most favored states of this country and of the world—those who died within seven years had contributed to the public support less than half, or only 46 per cent. of what is done in the best conditions of life." ("Fifth Report of Mass. Board of Health.")

It is equally true from a mere business standpoint that every child's casket put in the ground represents a considerable waste which affects not only the parents but the nation. There is no doubt about the loss in poor families where it is often necessary to go into debt to pay the funeral expenses; but the cost of maintaining the child while it lives and of tending to it during sickness practically amounts to a dead loss to the community at large, if death occurs before the time when it can become a working member. Sickly, deformed and idiotic children that become the wards of the state are a direct and appreciable burden, and the aggregate is a large item of the tax levy.

Mr. Hero Jewel, in arguing against the restriction of numbers, says: "Taking the preservation and progress of the species as the objects to which all else must be subordinated, we would say that the best function of the individual is to rear the largest number of the healthiest and most elevated offspring from birth to maturity," but he follows this up with the statement that "it is clearly a burden instead of a benefit when children are born who die before their product is an equivalent of their consumption, whatever allowance may be set off for the development of exertion and of sympathy in others." A German medical periodical, called The Doctor, in May, 1878, contained the following:

It is rather too low than too high an estimate, that of the 1,714,000 children born annually there is a loss of 30 per cent. of deaths during the first year of life, so that thus 514,000 are born every year in Germany only to leave the world at once, and these for the most part in a lamentable way. If we could arrive at this point that, instead of 40 births there were but 30, and instead of 30 deaths only 20 in every 1,000 persons, the annual increase would remain unaltered; but in the place of a diseased condition of domestic life there would ensue a healthy one, and one of the ugliest features of German life would disappear.

Dr. Baker, of Michigan, has shown that of children born of American parents the mortality is very decidedly less than of an equal number of children born of foreign parentage; Dr. Bowditch, of Massachusetts, has found that the former are taller, heavier and receive a better education than the latter, and the statistics of every state show less children born of American than of foreign parents.

In a report to the State Board of Charities, Dr. A. N. Bell wrote: "The child population under five years of age is 118 per 1,000, and of this large ratio 80 per cent.

are found in the tenements of the poor, and of these in some of the worst districts scarcely half survive to their second birthday. In these places multitudes of children are brought into the world by feeble and diseased parents, apparently for no other purpose than to sicken and die; but still many puny ones survive, and the more children in such places the more orphans and paupers."

### Why Little Children Die.

Dr. H. H. Vernon of England, in a lecture entitled, "Why Little Children Die," finds it easy to prove that "a terrible waste of infant life is going on among us." He says "that experience on a large scale has shown that infant mortality is practically reducible to ten per cent.; that it is therefore our duty as sanitarians, as citizens and as parents above all, not to rest until we have brought the infant mortality down to a reasonable standard." He does not respect the opinion of those who look complacently on large infantile mortality and talk about "compensations, natural selection and the survival of the fittest," solacing themselves with the thought that "the individual perishes, but the race flourishes." Dr. Vernon says "it is by no means certain that the sickliest die or the fittest survive. It is quite certain however, that all who are attacked by the diseases which kill are so much the worse for the attack, and not a few spoiled for all the active purposes of life. If only those born feeble and sickly were attacked by disease, and only the feeble and sickly died, then, from a point of view not more elevated than that of a breeder of stock, one might say that the weeding out of the sickly and feeble was an advantage to the remainder; but this is not the way the problem works. The true procession of events is that all are equally subjected to a number of conditions hostile to health and life; that some die; some do not die, but are maimed forever;

some have the seeds of future disease planted in them, and very few, if any, escape altogether. A population born and reared amidst conditions hostile to infant life is not in any sense a picked or weeded population, but a damaged and degenerating population, which is only saved from extinction by the constant influx of vigorous lives from healthier districts."

Dr. Alexander Wilder has written as follows:

There are certain laws, not very well understood, perhaps, which materially obviate the effects of extraordinary fecundity. In countries where a population is crowded, births are generally less numerous, and when they exceed a certain ratio they are pretty sure to be attended by an increased rate of mortality. For example, some years ago a traveler noticing the extraordinary profligacy of women in a Russian town, inferred that before long the excess of population would assure Russian preponderance over all Europe. A Swiss writer on political economy taking the matter in hand, discovered that an extraordinary death rate was also a peculiarity of the Russian village; so that a Swiss town of similar size, where the women produced fewer children, actually made a larger numerical increase of population. Even here in the City of New York, where Americans have notoriously small families, and where abortion is regularly practised, does not detract from social position, the mortality of children of Irish and German parentage is fearfully disproportionate    *Half of all who are born die before five years old. *The ill care of children is as notorious and as wicked as their murder before birth.* Besides, so far as cities are concerned, they are always human slaughter-houses. No city in history ever was able to exist by the generations of children born and reared in it, but always depended on recruiting from the country.

### Fewer and Better Children Wanted.

Anyone looking about the streets of New York city and counting "the babies on our block," would be apt to conclude that the inhabitants of this city were sufficiently prolific, but the most accurate vital statistics furnished by the Board of Health show that the number of deaths exceed the births by 5,000 yearly, and that of the 30,000 children born here nearly a third pass away in their first year, and full half die before the fifth year. During the next fifteen years the loss is much smaller, so that of the 30,000 born in any one year from ten to twelve thousand are likely to live to the age of twenty with a chance of becoming active and useful members of society. This item, the loss to this city of 60 per cent. of its population before maturity, before reaching the productive period, is an important one for the consideration of political economists, and for those who maintain that numbers are wanted irrespective of quality. Instead of thirty children born with a net result at the end of twenty years of twelve living ones, it would be far better that there should be only fifteen born, and these so well cared for that twelve would survive. Under conditions which would save twelve out of fifteen, these twelve would be far more likely to attain health, strength and longevity, and enjoy a life satisfactory to themselves and productive to the state, than the twelve which at the age of twenty constitute the remnant of thirty births originally; for as Dr. Vernon says, the influences which lead to the premature demise of 60 per cent. are harmful to the other 40 per cent., which survives. Of the latter no small percentage is maimed for life, left crippled, blind, deaf, idiotic, insane or hopelessly diseased and infirm by the bad influences which they have just managed to live through.

### Waste of Wealth.

In an address by the writer given at a Convention of the Institute of Heredity, held Dec. 8, 1881, the following argument was made concerning the relative value of pigs and babies:—"Let us consider the relation of this subject to political and business economy. Not long ago the Scientific American alluded to the excitement caused by the unusual mortality among hogs, and the quick action taken by the Government to investigate the cause, at the same time commenting upon the

fact that a similar increase of mortality among babies
frequently occurred in large cities without exciting any
great commotion. According to the report of the Bu-
reau of Vital Statistics, 17,000 children under five years
of age died in New York during the past year! Babies
are not an article of commerce here; but they are nevertheless related to dollars and cents, and strange it is
that this is not more understood. One family there was
that did not lose sight of it. They caused to be inscribed on the tombstone of their *dear* departed the following touching and instructive lines:

> Our little Johnny's gone to praise,
> He neither cries nor hollers,
> He lived but five and thirty days,
> And cost us forty dollars.

And they got off cheap too! Children who come into
the world only to wither away and die, are a direct loss,
in a business way, to their parents. They are often an
entirely unnecessary expense that families in moderate
circumstances can ill afford. If they are born crippled
in body or mind they eventually become a burden to the
state, perhaps to the extent of thousands of dollars before they are finally buried at public expense in the potter's field. Is this a cruel and unfeeling way to speak of
these unfortunates? If life were any boon to them it
might be. The state suffers loss to support them, but
they are more to be pitied than the state. Therefore,
we plead against the reproduction of such unfortunates,
first, for their own sake, second, for the economy of the
state. Everywhere the cost of charities and correction
is, year after year, mounting higher, and those who
supervise them see that under the existing order of
things this is likely to continue. Present methods seem
as hopeless as fighting the mythical dragon when two
heads sprang up where one was cut off. The time is

fast approaching when other means than those now in vogue must be discovered for dealing with the hydra-headed monsters, crime, pauperism and disease."

"Brick" Pomeroy, in a series of papers entitled, "Pen Pictures of Things As They Are," describing his visits among the Island Institutions belonging to New York, truly echoes the refrain that "one half the world knows nothing of how the other half lives," in these words: "Not one-tenth of those who form the resident population of New York city know the one-fourth of what is going on here in the matter of charities, corrections and educational efforts. In the office of a well-known attorney of national reputation, I asked:

"'What is done with the idiotic children born in this city?'

"'Strangled, I presume; never gave the subject a thought.'

"And yet there is a place in this city where there are more than two hundred idiots and feeble-minded folk, all kindly cared for and forming a part of the fifteen thousand population comprising the criminals and eleemosynaries cared for by the Department of Public Charities and Corrections, without which New York would be a hell of high degree."

The penal, reformatory and charitable public institutions of the State of New York are an expense to its treasury of over ten millions yearly, and probably the tax upon its people for private institutions and charity associations, of which there are several hundred, would amount to another ten million of dollars yearly. It would, of course, be preposterous to attribute all this necessity of expense to any one cause; but it is doubtful if any one thing would do more to reduce it than the limitation of the reproduction of paupers, criminals and that shiftless, reckless and vicious class that keep on reproducing themselves in spite of the fact that they would prefer to avoid so doing if conveniently possible.

It therefore appears that, besides great waste of life, there is immense waste of resources, loss of national wealth, necessitating extra burden upon the industrious, self-supporting classes, because of the continuance of this "go-as-you-please" custom of propagation. When tax-payers, who are made up of the industrious people remaining outside of public and charitable institutions, become fully awakened to the enormous expense of supporting the inmates of such institutions together with a large number of shiftless, good-for-nothing-but-breeding-and-not-even-that people who remain at large, they will more earnestly seek a remedy.

# CHAPTER III.

## Scientific Philanthropy Finds the Radical Remedy in Regulation of Reproduction.

Don Piatt, a caustic commentator on political affairs, has said "no people ever indulged in any reform until their stomachs or backs, or both, began to feel the oppression;" but those who most directly feel the oppression of increasing taxes do sometimes arouse themselves "to take action against a sea of troubles and by opposing, end them." This year (1885) brings new incentive for such action in New York city where the tax-rate has been raised from 2.25 to 2.40, an increase reported to be due in part to the growing expense of the "judicial" department. But the burden of State expenses is not borne ultimately by those who pay cash directly into the public treasury; eventually and inevitably it falls largely upon the industrious working classes—the rent-payers of the tenement house population—and thus they are made to suffer indirectly the cost, as well as directly the discomforts of their ignorance and recklessness. Mr. Charles F. Wingate, a philanthropist by nature, a sanitary engineer by profession and a practical observer of the "night-side" of city life, early in the year 1885, wrote for the New York Tribune an article on "The

Tenement Problem," declaring prompt and vigorous action necessary and offering practical suggestions. From it we select a few of the best:

### Help the Poor to Help Themselves.

"Whenever the sufferings of the poor are described it will be suggested that it is the duty of the State to interfere in their behalf. The best authorities are, however, opposed to Government directly assisting the poor except in seasons of exceptional distress. There is too much risk of pauperizing them and of establishing a bad precedent. The true principle of State action is to enforce stricter laws regulating the building, plumbing and drainage of tenements." The benefits already gained by sanitary regulations justify extending their scope and enforcing them more rigidly. Boards of health have already accomplished much in the way of removing nuisances, but they should be encouraged to do still more. "We must stop the erection of old-fashioned double-deckers; we must weed out the most dilapidated and unsanitary houses; we must strictly enforce the sanitary code; we must lay out summer parks; we must have public baths in winter as well as in summer."

Thus he goes on advocating good measures, more rapid-transit to reach the suburbs, more primary education of children, technical schools, less liquor shops, better sewers, cleaner streets, pure and sufficient water supply, an abundance of good milk, etc.; and he further says "we need fewer agencies for doling alms and more societies for helping the poor to help themselves. The masses require less coal and grocery tickets and more of human sympathy and counsel."

Mr. Wingate nowhere intimates that this personal counsel would include a recommendation to limit the

number of offspring, though he regards the over-crowding of tenements as their worst feature, and proposes
that these people should be restricted in the privilege
of taking lodgers into families which are already too
crowded, or into houses over-"crammed." He remarks
that these people are reckless and slovenly, that they
destroy property, waste water and are negligent in their
disposal of garbage; and it is probably only the ordinary rules of cleanliness and sanitation which he would
impart by personal counsel; but to an ordinary observer
their recklessness in the matter of reproduction is the
most evident cause of over-crowding, and in the light of
results must be regarded as the worst feature of their
recklessness. Dr. Charles R. Drysdale, a member of
the Royal College of Physicians, of London, says:

"My professional life has been among hospitals for
many years, and that has led me into contact with the
poor of this city. I have been obliged to see what a
miserable condition of squalor there is, of utter distress
and indigence. I have been continually obliged to
lament the excessive rapidity with which the poorer
classes bring unfortunate children into the world, who,
in consequence, die, or grow up rickety and weak. Sir
William Jenner, long Physician to the Children's Hospital, has written well on the subject; and he used to
say, what my experience has confirmed, that, when a
working man marries, the first one or two children look
healthy, whilst the third will be rickety, because the
mother is not able to give it the proper nourishment
which she lacks herself. Rickets is a great cause of
death in London, much greater than is generally supposed. The death-rate is enormous where families are
large among the poorer classes. * * * Hence if children are born in great numbers among the poor, they
are simply born to die. In my hospital experience in

London, I continually observe women suckling their
young for eighteen months or upward to prevent another birth. This is most injurious to both mother and
child. The poor mothers are often worn to death by
large families, and often fall into consumption from this
cause. Then it is most common to see mothers among
the poor who have had fifteen children alive, and only
two or three of which survive the starvation and misery of
their home. To bring so many children into the world,
as many do, seems to me the greatest social crime a person
can commit, and I look upon it as worse than drunkenness or other physical excess."

The above was part of the testimony given by
D͟r. Drysdale when called as a witness in the prosecution
of Mr. Bradlaugh and Mrs. Besant for publishing Dr.
Knowlton's "Fruits of Philosophy."

### Discourage Reckless Propagation.

Is it not, therefore, appropriate to suggest that when
the inspectors appointed by the Board of Health, and
the agents of amateur or voluntary Sanitary Aid Societies, go out upon their missionary work in the "slums,"
they should go prepared not only to give instruction,
distribute tracts and apply the laws of the "Sanitary
Code," but also to discourage amongst these people that
recklessness in propagation which it would be easy to
demonstrate to them is the cause of a large share of
their misery. Mr. Wingate says "a strict enforcement
of the Sanitary Code would accomplish wonders," and
also "agitation and appeals to enlightened self-interest
will do much." Outside of all moral considerations and
arguments based upon the public good there are enough
facts and arguments in the line of their own self-
interests which might be made the basis of appeals to
these people, urging them to make an effort toward
reform in this matter.

Of course, any general appeal of this sort, unaccompanied by further advice regarding ways and means, would be like seed falling upon stony ground—bearing little fruit of good.   Now comes in the difficulty.   Here is where roads divide—opinions differ.   Among the large class of people who would concede at once the immorality of reckless propagation, who would accept as axiomatic the statement that no one has a right to bring a child into the world without some fair prospect of providing for its support, or who would assert that persons seriously diseased in mind and body ought to refrain from becoming parents,—among such thinkers there is a broad difference of opinion as to how these immoralities are to be avoided, but these will be studied and compared in the following chapters, while this one is a little lengthened to include a few remarks from high sources upon the immorality of reckless propagation— irresponsible parentage.   The following extract is from John Morley's "Life of Rousseau :"

### Irresponsible Parentage.

"There is assuredly no word to be said by any one with firm reason and unsophisticated conscience in extenuation of this crime.   Let Rousseau be a little free from excessive reproach from all clergymen, sentimentalists and others who do their worst to uphold the common and rather bestial opinion in favor of reckless propagation, and who, if they do not advocate the despatch of children to public institutions, still encourage a selfish incontinence which ultimately falls in burdens on others than the offenders, and which turns the family into a scene of squalor and brutishness, producing a kind of parental influence that is far more disastrous and demoralizing than the absence of it in public institutions can possibly be.   If the propagation

of children without regard to their maintenance be
either a virtue or a necessity, and if afterwards the only
alternatives are their maintenance in an asylum on the
one hand, and their maintenance in the degredation of
a poverty-stricken home on the other, we should not
hesitate to give people who acted as Rousseau acted all
that credit for self-denial and high moral courage which
he so audaciously claimed for himself. It is certainly
no more criminal to produce children with the deliberate intention of abandoning them to public charity, as
Rousseau did, than it is to produce them in deliberate
reliance on the besotted maxim that 'He who sends
mouths will send meat,' or any other of the spurious
saws which make Providence do duty for self-control
and add to the gratification of physical appetite the
grotesque luxury of religious unction."

Matthew Arnold, a good scholar and deep reasoner, a
man of culture, of tenderness, and broad, wide charity
and benevolent feeling, says:

A man's children are not really *sent* any more than the pictures
upon his wall, or the horses in his stable are *sent;* and to bring
people into the world when one cannot afford to keep them and
one's self decently and not too precariously, or to bring more of
them into the world than one can afford to keep thus, is by no
means an accomplishment of the divine will or a fulfillment of
Nature's simplest laws.

The following extract from a sermon preached in
London, in aid of the Poor Clergy Relief Association, by
Dr. Fraser, Bishop of Manchester, deserves reproduc-
tion. The Bishop said:

Clergymen involved themselves in domestic responsibilities some
of which they might have postponed, and some of which never
ought to have been made. He had been called a very hard-hearted
Bishop because in his primary charge he felt it his duty to say that
in the exercise of his patronage he could not consider the fact that
a man who had married and got a family around him, had established a claim upon him. He should say to a man who had married
and whose wife was bearing children year after year, 'Don't come

to me for preferment on that account. Do your work, and do it with all your heart, and then say, "Bishop, have you anything to give me, not because I have a wife and children with whom I recklessly involved myself, but because I have done my duty?'" And to that man he should reply: 'Because you have done your duty I will forget the recklessness to which you refer.'

The following comments on Dr. Fraser's sermon are by Mrs. Annie Besant:

What does Dr. Fraser mean? He seems to distinguish between two sets of actions, responsibilities which "might be postponed," and others which "ought never to have been made." The first clearly applies to marriage; to what does the second, which is not marriage, refer? Does it, as would seem from the phrase as to the wife, refer to voluntary limitation of the family? If not, to what does it refer? Does the Bishop wish to preach the celibacy of the clergy? If not, what does he recommend? The celibacy of the clergy has been productive of the very grossest immorality in every country where it has prevailed. The honest Bishop of Manchester cannot be recommending this historically-discredited theory. Does he then find himself in the dilemma: early marriage and large family—poverty; delayed marriage—immorality; early marriage and limitation of the family being the only course left? If this be the Bishop's meaning, ought he not, from his place in the House of Lords, to ask why Edward Truelove is in gaol for teaching what he himself preaches from the pulpit? and ought he not to aid us in annulling the law under which we were indicted?

In the Popular Science Monthly of August, 1884, may be found an article on "Scientific Philanthropy," which as a whole might be appropriately quoted here, but because of its length only the main argument in a few selections can be given. The author of this essay, Mr. Lee J. Vance, B.S., writes in opposition to the modern "sentimental" philanthropy charging that "the whole tendency of the system is to encourage the increase of pauperism and crime. It has been a great waste of money, effort and sympathy—has been the means of diffusing habits of improvidence, idleness and servility in the poorer classes. To aid the good-for-nothings to multiply, says Mr. Spencer, is the same as maliciously providing for our descendants a multitude

of enemies. All modern philanthropic legislation has
relied upon palliatives; it has undoubtedly ameliorated
the near effects of poverty, but unquestionably it has
failed to remove its remote causes. Philanthropy should
be established upon a definite and exact scientific basis.
In his address before the Academy in 1880, Victor Sar-
dou said that sympathy impelled men to apply a remedy
before they ascertained the cause of the disease—to
trust in the efficacy of panaceas rather than in the *vis
medicatrix*. This he called sentimental philanthropy.
The conscious aim of scientific philanthropy is in the
first place to deal with the struggle of man with nature
--is to help men to help themselves; secondly its aim is
to regulate the struggle of man with man—is to help
men to understand and adapt themselves to the conditions of existence. * * * * The principle of selection, with the survival of the fittest, encourages the
multiplication of those persons best fitted for the conditions of life, by carrying off the weak and sickly who
are least fitted for those conditions; and if left to work
without check, it would result in the slow and steady
improvement of the individual faculties and race characteristics by purifying the blood, invigorating the
energies and strengthening the social instincts. But
we civilized men, says Mr. Darwin, do our utmost to
check the process of elimination; we build asylums for
the imbecile, the maimed and the sick; we institute
poor laws, and our physicians exert their utmost skill to
save the life of every patient to the last moment. The
effect of the survival of all those who would be elim-
inated by the principle of selection, together with the
rapid rate of increase of the reckless and degraded over
the stronger and better members is to increase the pres-
sure of population on the means of subsistence. This
it is which gives rise to the so-called social problem.
Scientific philanthropy, therefore, is the most modern

attempt to deal with this problem, which began in primeval times, because of man's rapid multiplication, and which will continue as long as civilization continues. * * * * It is difficult, therefore, to exaggerate the harm caused by the artificial preservation of the feeblest upon the physical status of future generations.

* * * What Mr. Spencer claims, and what is claimed on behalf of scientific philanthropy, is simply to regulate, by healthy and moral modes, the increase of improvident on the means of subsistence, and this the true philanthropist will do by teaching the laws of health, by right physical education and by wise sanitary measures."

Mr. Vance and the eminent persons whose names are given in the preceding paragraphs, thus give their endorsement to the proposition that we must devise means to regulate reproduction--to check reckless propagation  but they apparently prefer to deal in generalities and to avoid particulars, which is not a very practical and thoroughly scientific method. Their opinions are valuable, so far as they go, but we must look to other, bolder and more outspoken writers for practical suggestions of ways and means.

# CHAPTER IV.

## Regulation of Reproduction—How it may be Effected,

WHEN the advocates of regulation of reproduction in the human race are asked, "What is to be done," by what means is this important matter to be controlled, they must, almost of necessity, reply favoring one of the following propositions:

*First.*—Celibacy and deferred marriage, as advocated by Rev. Mr. Malthus in his book, "The Law of Population."

*Second.*—Continence in marriage, except when offspring is desired, as advocated by the Alpha, a monthly journal edited by Mrs. Dr. Caroline B. Winslow, at Washington, D. C.

*Third.*—"Conjugal prudence" by the aid of certain "preventive checks," the remedy of the Neo-Malthusian philosophy, as advocated by many philanthropists and physicians in Europe and America.

## Self-Limitation of Evils.

Before comparing the relative merits and practicability of the three possible methods of regulating reproduction, let us inquire how far and in what ways population checks are already operative. They are now operating in direct and indirect ways; by strictly

natural and by artificial methods.   It is an interesting
and suggestive fact that nature herself puts a limit to
reproduction of human ills.   Both men and women are
rendered sterile through diseases affecting the nervous
system, the blood and the procreative organs, as well
as because of mere physical degeneracy.   Thus nature
handicaps these evils, and it is perhaps largely due to
this fact that man has made some progress.

It is also true that where nature does not absolutely
put her interdict upon reproduction, the child of ill-
conditioned parents is either prematurely born or still-
born, or it will be likely to die of inherited weakness or
disease before reaching the reproductive period.   Thus,
what is from one point of view a frightful infant mortality is from another standpoint a safe and beneficent
provision of Nature.   Furthermore, if in any family of
marked evil tendencies the first and second generation
succeed in living to the reproductive age, it is nevertheless true that the sins of the father are visited upon
the children to the third and fourth generation of them
that hate Go(o)d, and in a short time (according to
Nature's account of time) that family is dropped out.
It is frequently remarked that the nobility of England
is dying out and that the House of Lords cannot recruit
itself from scions of its own household.   New peers
must be created to supply the vacant places.   Haeckel
says, ''It is in reigning families that mental disorders
are hereditary in an unusual degree.   This phenomenon
can scarcely surprise us if we consider what injury
these privileged classes inflict upon themselves by their
unnatural, one-sided education, and their artificial sep-
aration from the rest of mankind.''   Unnatural vices
and luxuries operate perhaps even more evidently upon
the wealthy classes to cut them off from inheriting the
earth than do the miseries of the poor, and the gospel

of moderation in all things needs to be proclaimed to the one class as much as to the other.

Many of the social evils have a tendency to self-limitation through the operation of cause and effect. Drunkenness often impairs the reproductive power and inclination. Pauperism, uncleanliness and squalor seem to be no hindrance to prolific child bearing; but they have their inevitable attendants, such as zymotic and other infantile diseases, which in some districts take off more than half the children that are born before they are five years old—maybe a fourth or a half during the first year.

Observing these various means by which Nature herself sets a limit to increase of evils through propagation, the question arises how far it may be admissable to assist or displace her in so doing by artificial means of our own device. Thus, we pass from the consideration of natural or positive checks to prudential checks or restraint, to inquire to what extent artificial restraint is already in vogue, directly or indirectly, enforced and voluntary, by individuals, families and states.

### State Restraint of Reproduction.

The state has established penal and reformatory institutions, asylums for the insane and inebriates, not, of course, with any direct intention of restraining the reproduction of these classes, but that is one result of committing them to the care of state institutions, so that every insane, drunken or criminal member of the community who is thus disposed of for a number of years has at least that much shortening of his or her reproductive period. This must be regarded as one form of enforced artificial restraint upon reckless propagation; but the history of the Juke family, as related by Mr. R. L. Dugdale when a member of the prison association, shows how far it is from being a sufficient protection against the rapid reproduction of criminals, paupers and their derivatives. It was traced out by pains-taking research that from one woman called Margaret, who, like Topsey, merely "growed" without pedigree, as a pauper in a village on the upper Hudson, about eighty-five years ago, there descended 673 children, grand-children and great-grandchildren, of whom 200 were criminals of the dangerous class, 280 adult paupers and 50 prostitutes, while 300 children of her lineage died prematurely. The last fact proves to what extent in this family nature was kind to the rest of humanity in saving it from a still larger aggregation of undesirable and costly members, for it is estimated that the expense to the State of the descendants of Maggie was over a million and a quarter dollars; and the State itself did something also toward preventing a greater expense by the restraint exercised upon the criminals, paupers and idiots of the family during a considerable portion of their lives.

There is a sort of enforced restraint upon population affecting the individual when from inability to take upon himself the support of a family he remains celi-bate, when his preference would be to marry and have a family. So celibacy may even be regarded as an en-forced artificial restraint upon propagation. There is also a voluntary form of celibacy operating toward the same result, and another phase of the same sort of re-straint appears in married life where strict continence is adhered to, either from purely personal motives or from pecuniary reasons.

### Malthus' Remedy—Deferred Marriage.

After Malthus has described how all vice and misery operate as positive checks to population, he recommends moral restraint, such as celibacy, deferred marriage and marital continence as remedies against Nature's cruel positive checks; and he discountenances without further specification than the phrase "improper arts," a class of checks which he calls vicious checks. He writes (page 280, of volume II): "There are, perhaps, few actions which tend so directly to diminish the general happiness as to marry without the means of supporting children. * * * It appears, therefore, that it is within the power of each individual to avoid all the evil consequences to himself and society resulting from the principle of population by the practice of a virtue clearly dictated to him by the light of Nature, and expressly enjoined in revealed religion." Malthus was a clergyman as well as a philosopher, and he wrote in 1826 when it was far more common to appeal to revealed religion than to the facts of science for the decision of questions in morals, and when indeed there were far less facts in science to appeal to than at present; but on the whole I think he made it plainer that the virtue of continence is dictated by the "light of Nature" than by "revealed religion." I can remember more distinctly the injunction, "Increase and multiply and replenish the earth," than anything in Scripture to the contrary.

### Prevention and Abortion Contrasted.

Malthus too hastily passed over a class of prudential preventive checks by merely calling them vicious and improper arts, though perhaps he was right concerning all the arts of which he had knowledge, one of which was abortion; but since his time physiological science has made great progress, and we are now able to see distinctly the difference between the mere prevention of conception and the forcible interference with the product of conception, which constitutes abortion. There is a distinction and a difference of great importance, and one which persons who lack instruction in the physiology of reproduction, are pretty sure to overlook. The

origin of a new life is effected by what is called the process of conception, which requires the coming together
under proper conditions of the microscopically small
male and female elements—called respectively the
sperm-cell and the ovule. These objects are so small
that they must be magnified one hundred times in order
to be seen at all; but the joining of two such minute elements effects impregnation or conception, and the result
is the beginning of a new organism in what is called
the product of conception. Any interference with the
natural growth and development of this germ of life at
any stage of its uterine life causes an abortion, and is
therefore destructive of a living entity; but if the two
elements necessary to conception fail to come together
there is no impregnation, no beginning of a new life,
and physiologically speaking, there is no sin in merely
preventing the union of the two microscopic elements
by artificial means which for want of a single appropriate
word, I will call contraceptics—a new coinage literally
meaning, against-beginning—or something to oppose or
prevent a beginning by conception. Thus, we make
clear the distinction between contraceptics which prevent conception and abortives which interfere with the
actual living product of conception, and here the line is
drawn between celibacy and infanticide. On the one
side of this line we have enforced penal restraint, celibacy, continence and contraceptics, and on the other
side of the line abortion, infanticide and all the positive
natural population checks which Malthus wrote about.

From this time our attention will be directed to the
methods on the contraceptic side of the line. A study
of methods of prevention of conception in their relation
to sexual hygiene will show that while there can be no
harm in the prevention of access of the two elements
above described, however effected, there may be objection to some methods either from the light of sexual

physiology or because of social and moral considerations.

The Rev. Mr. Malthus advocated, as we have seen, moral restraint in the form of celibacy, deferred marriage and continence, but these are in the light of later science found to be objectionable for two main reasons.

### Celibacy "Easier Said than Done."

In the first place, celibacy when of the enforced kind, is seldom lived up to. There is a putative celibacy which does not mean the practice of strict continence, but which permits to itself certain laxity, irregularity or promiscuity in sex relations, and this sort of putative celibacy is objectionable as a prudential check: first, because it often is no check, as evidenced by the fact that in some European cities nearly half the births are illegitimate children, and secondly, because where it does operate as a check it is mainly at the expense of health and morals—one inevitable result being the social evil. Malthus says: "It is clearly the duty of each individual not to marry till he has a prospect of supporting children, and the interval between the age of puberty and the age at which each individual might venture to marry must be passed in strict chastity, because the law of chastity cannot be violated without producing evil." He, and others who have followed him in this line, may expound the beauties of chastity as a moral virtue and a public benefit; but however many amens echo from the hearers when in a religious mood, it appears that practically the injunction to strict continence does not influence conduct to any greater extent than in his own time—sixty years ago.

John Christien, secretary of the midnight meeting movement in London, a man who has spent thirty years in reclaiming prostitutes, says: "I would have

all young persons bound together in wedlock if it could
be done decently and legally, before they were out of
their teens, and I care not if at first they have a hard
struggle to support themselves; for it is better to struggle against want than to be doomed to an unequal and
mostly unsuccessful struggle with youthful passions."
Mr. Christien has seen the practical or worldly side of
life, and his observation does not encourage him to take
as hopeful a view as Malthus did of the possibility of
making moral restraint a practical population check
among the masses of mankind. It therefore appears
that deferred marriage practically results in an increased birth of "natural" children, thus failing to be
a check upon population, vice and misery; or it predis-
poses to some of the worst moral evils and the spread of
the most virulent and pernicious contagious diseases
through lapses from virtue in the form of promiscuity
and prostitution

### Strict Celibacy Unphysiological.

True celibacy, continence or chastity does operate as a
contraceptic population check, but is objectionable because not physiological. Statistics are frequently quoted
to prove that marriage conduces to health and longevity,
but such statistics will not be employed here for the very
good reason that there are no statistics concerning any
large number of persons of whom it can be assumed
that they live strictly celibate lives. It is not difficult
to get at the facts about the mortality rate of married
people, but where are we to obtain for comparison the
tables indicating conditions as to health and disease of
strictly celibates as a class? This question of the physiological effect of celibacy can at present only be studied
in individual cases, and numerous recorded observations of competent physicians prove that strict continence may be, has been and often is the cause of ser-

ious ill-health; that celibacy is a disregard of natural law, and cannot receive the endorsement of science as a harmless contraceptic.

I quote again from Malthus: "However powerful may be the impulses of passion, they are generally in some degree modified by reason, and it does not seem entirely visional to suppose that if the true and permanent cause of poverty were clearly explained and forcibly brought home to each man's bosom, it would have some and perhaps not an inconsiderable influence on his conduct; at least the experiment has never yet been fairly tried." While thus earnest and hopeful in the enunciation of his remedy for poverty, vice and misery, he was not unaware of its being an unpleasant prescription which he was writing for his fellow-men, for which Christian resignation in the fulfilment of duty and the avoidance of worse misfortunes were offered as sufficient recompense. He recognized the beneficent influences of the dominant passion, and wrote thus of it:

Considering then the passion between the sexes in all its bearings and relations, and including the enduring engagement of parent and child resulting from it, few will be disposed to deny that it is one of the principal ingredients of human happiness. * * * A careful attention to the remote as well as immediate effects of all the human passions and of the general laws of nature leads us strongly to the conclusion that, under the present situation of things, few or none of them will admit of being greatly diminished without narrowing the sources of good more powerfully than the sources of evil. And the reason is obvious. They are in fact the materials of all our pleasures as well as our pains; of all our happiness as well as of all our misery; of all our virtues as well as of all our vices. It must therefore be regulation and direction that are wanted, not diminution or extinction.

### Neo-Malthusian Philosophy.

Many philosophic thinkers since his time have adopted Malthus' idea of the law of population, but have discarded his remedy, believing that the objects stated in the last quotation from him can be far better achieved by the employment of prudential checks in marriage; and as this remedy renders possible the regulation of propagation without actually diminishing the natural sources of happiness, it is more reasonable to suppose that it will prove acceptable to mankind in general, appeal to reason and influence conduct, than the Malthusian remedy which in sixty years has proven itself to be more visionary than practicable.

Mr. John Stuart Mill has stated what is called the *Neo-Malthusian Philosophy* in his principles of political economy, from which I quote at some length:

Civilization in every one of its aspects is a struggle against the animal instincts; over some, even of the strongest of them, it has shown itself capable of acquiring abundant control. It has artificialized large portions of mankind to such an extent that of many of their most natural inclinations, they have scarcely a vestige or remembrance left. If it has not brought the instinct of population under as much restraint as is needful, we must remember that it has never seriously tried. What efforts it has made have mostly been in a contrary direction. Religion, morality and statesmanship have vied with one another in incitement to marriage, and to the multiplication of the species so it be but in wedlock.

Religion has not even yet discontinued its encouragement. The Roman Catholic clergy (of any other clergy it is unnecessary to speak, since none other have any considerable influence over the poorer classes) everywhere think it their duty to promote marriage in order to prevent fornication. There is still in many minds a strong religious prejudice against the true doctrine. The rich, provided the consequences do not touch themselves, think it impugns the wisdom of Providence to suppose that misery can result from the operation of a natural propensity; the poor think that God never sends mouths but he sends meat. No one would guess from the language of either that man had any voice or choice in the matter.

So complete is the confusion of ideas on the whole subject, owing in a great degree to the mystery in which it is shrouded by a spurious delicacy, which prefers that right and wrong should be mismeasured and confounded on one of the subjects most momentous to human welfare rather than the subject should be freely spoken of and discussed. People are little aware of the cost to mankind of this scrupulosity of speech. *The diseases of society can no more than corporal maladies be prevented or cured without being spoken*

*about in plain language.* All experience shows that the mass of
mankind never judge of moral questions for themselves, never see
anything to be right or wrong until they have been frequently told
it; and who tells them that they have any duties in the matter in
question while they keep within matrimonial limits? Who meets
with the smallest condemnation, or rather who does not meet with
sympathy and benevolence for any amount of evil which he may
have brought on himself and those dependent on him by this
species of incontinence? While a man who is intemperate in
drink is discountenanced and despised by all who profess to be
moral people, it is one of the chief grounds made use of in appeals
to the benevolent that the applicant has a large family and is unable to maintain them. Little improvement can be expected in
morality until the producing large families is regarded with the
same feelings as drunkenness or any other physical excess. But
whilst the aristocracy and clergy are foremost to set the example of
this species of incontinence, what can be expected from the poor?

This view has already been adopted in England by
Robert Owen, his son Robert Dale Owen, Prof. Leone
Levi, Charles Bradlaugh, Mrs. Annie Besant, and Dr.
C. R. Drysdale; and according to the statement of the
latter, his views are held by Sir Henry Thompson, Dr.
Hardwicke and Dr. Morell Mackenzie. One of the first
physicians of this country to recommend conjugal prudence was Dr. Knowlton, of Massachusetts, who, about
fifty years ago, suffered imprisonment for his advanced
ideas. It was his pamphlet upon which was instituted
the prosecution of Mr. Bradlaugh and Mrs. Besant, and
toward the end of that remarkable trial the charge to
the jury, delivered by Lord Chief Justice Cockburn, revealed that he was certainly inclined to favor the ideas
advocated by Knowlton, Bradlaugh and Besant. This
is his summing up of the case:

Malthus suggested years ago— and his suggestions have been supported by economists since his time—that the only possible way of
keeping down population was by retarding marriage to as late a
period as possible; the argument being that the fewer the marriages
the fewer would be the people. But another class of theorists say
that that remedy is bad, and possibly worse than the disease; because, though you might delay marriage you cannot restrain those
instincts which are implanted in human nature, and that people

will have the gratification and satisfaction of passions powerfully implanted; if not in one way in some other, so you have evils of prostitution substituted for the evils of over-population. Now, what says Dr. Knowlton? "There being this choice of evils—there being the unquestioned evil of over-population, which exists in a great part of the civilized world—is the remedy proposed by Malthus so doubtful that it would probably lead to greater evils than the one it was intended to remedy?" Dr. Knowlton suggests—and here we come to the critical point of this inquiry—he suggests that instead of marriage being postponed, it should be hastened. He suggests that marriage should take place in the hey day of life when the passions are at their highest, and that the evils of over-population shall be remedied by persons after they have married, having recourse to artificial means to prevent the procreation of a numerous offspring, and the consequent evils, especially to the poorer classes, which the production of a too numerous offspring is certain to bring about.

This quotation is taken from Dr. C. R. Drysdale's pamphlet on "The Law of Population," in which he traces the discovery of the possibility of "conjugal prudence" to France, where Mr. Francis Place and Robert Owen went to learn of its methods and results. Guizot, the great French historian, says in his "History of Civilization" that "every great idea that has been born into the world in modern times has been born in France, or after its birth in some other country it has had to come to France to be fully elaborated and finished." It will be fair to admit that this idea originated in France, that it gave the incentive to many books in England, notably Richard Carlisle's "Every Woman's Book," Austin Holyoake's "Large or Small Families," and Robert Dale Owen's "Moral Physiology;" and the reading of the latter led Dr. Charles Knowlton, a Boston physician, to write the celebrated "Fruits of Philosophy," made celebrated in being the cause of criminal prosecution of the author in Massachusetts as well as of Mr. Bradlaugh and Mrs. Besant in England. The latter trial brought the subject to public notice more than any other one thing, and also resulted in a new and better statement of the whole matter, the evils of over-population and its remedy through conjugal prudence, based upon more recent knowledge, statistical, physiological and experimental, as presented in Mrs. Besant's pamphlet, entitled "The Law of Population: Its Consequences and its Bearing upon Human Conduct and Morals."

### Annie Besant's Bold Book.

Mrs. Besant, who displayed wonderful courage and rare talent in her own self-defense on the occasion of the trial, and was by the jury "exonerated from any corrupt motives in publishing" Dr. Knowlton's pamphlet, "held that to destroy life, after it once lives, is the most immoral doctrine that can be put forward; and that when a doctor goes to a man and tells him that his wife can never bear a living child, he ought to be able also to impart to him such physiological instructions as should prevent the occurrence of conception." In her own pamphlet she further says: "It is clearly useless to preach the limitation of the family, and to conceal the means whereby such limitation shall be effected. If the limitation be a duty it cannot be wrong to afford such information as shall enable people to discharge it." Therefore her book was made practically useful as well as argumentatively convincing, and it is undoubtedly the best writing upon the subject now extant in England or America, being the only recent and *instructive* one which has thus far escaped prosecution; but there is more practical physiological information to impart than was put into her book. So there is room for, as well as call for, an American book. It is probably true that if the idea of "conjugal prudence" was born in France it has received its most thorough study and elaboration in this country; and, indeed, the best mechanical means yet devised, though commonly described as a "French" article, was really invented and elaborated in the office of an American physician.

The physician here referred to is Dr. E. B. Foote, Sr., author of several popular medical and physiological works, and the staunch advocate for more than thirty years of making a substitution of conjugal prudence and preventive checks for the more cruel and positive checks on the other side of the line; but his advocacy of contraceptics has been mainly because they afford a means of regulating, as well as limiting, reproduction, making it possible for families to control the time and select the conditions which shall favor the production of healthy children. His writings frequently give proof of his conviction that where children are not wanted it is better on all accounts that they should not come as accidents and intruders, and on the other hand that there are enough persons who are desirous of having their due share of such "blessings" to afford a reasonable and healthful increase of population. Though he has not stood alone in the United States in stirpicultural propaganda urging the adapting of scientific principles of generation to the human race—he has certainly been one of the boldest and most persistent preachers of this New Gospel, while at the cost of much time, labor, money and reputation, he has maintained th t in order to inaugurate a reform in methods of human reproduction it is necessary to develop and make *available* contraceptic methods of regulation or control. This scheme for the physical improvement of humanity appears to be one of the comparatively new things under the sun—new enough, at all events, to provoke active opposition from some quarters (the hind quarters in the van of human progress)—and so many of its disciples are disinclined to take a bold stand and confess faith, but our friend M. M. (Brick) Pomeroy acknowledges his allegiance to the new gospel in no uncertain sounds.

## Pen Pictures of New York Life.

In the first of his series of Pen Pictures of New York Life, he writes: "Having thus started in on the trail of a waif, we shall follow it chapter by chapter from the womb to the tomb--from its birth in the lying-in ward of the hospital to the almshouse for the aged indigent, and then on to the potter's field; and by the time our chapters on this subject are completed we will be able to prove that the physician whose agencies can prevent conception stands at the head of the list of the great benefactors of mankind or humanity."

In a subsequent chapter under the sub-head of "Conclusions Reached," he speaks again in a similar way; thus: "The great first cause is the bringing into the world of offspring that have no business here, and whose conception had better have been prevented. A beetle-browed, bull-necked brute of a man and voter, is by a priest or politician for a dollar or so, united in wedlock to an ignorant female. The result is a babe. It is brought up under a cloud, brutally treated, and as an adult is exactly what it was made to be. The poor, starved, neglected wife is plastered over with quotations from Paul—"Wives submit yourselves unto your husbands." They may kick, scream, pray, entreat and implore, but this maker of a demand for little coffins, etc., tells the poor, sick, starved wife that she must multiply and replenish, when she is not fit to be multiplied from, and replenishes only the potter's field. The remedy for this is stirpiculture, and affording all wives or women who ask for it a preventive to conception. Not a tool or a medicine to *murder*, but a *prevention* to laying foundations in misery to grow up in misrule. Hell may be peopled but God is *not* glorified by compelling women to submit, to suffer, to stand in an ignorant religious pillory, to be delivered of disgraces to God, the Creator, or to humanity whose great ideal appears to be lost. Prevent conception of a crime or a criminal, and God and humanity are both served. Prevent the growth of mental nonentities and physical, and consequent mental weakness, and the human race is from that moment improved. If an eye offends thee, pluck it out. The educated, humane physician who will inform women how to escape compulsory child-bearing, will serve God, heaven and tax-payers better than they have been served lo! these many years. Merely breeding voters and paupers is not an evidence of wisdom or a way to progression."

In this country there are many humanitarians who unhesitatingly advocate borning better babies and avoiding the necessity of so many human repair shops, through controlling propagation; but perhaps the majority of those favorable to such ideas have as yet only expressed themselv.s tentatively, as for instance, Mrs. Isabel A. Beecher Hooker, who in a pamphlet, entitled "Womanhood: Its Sanctities and Fidelities," expres:es the opinion that "far worse misfortunes might befall our race than decreasing families, as long as children are born to such an inheritance as too many young men of the present day are likely to transmit." Rev. M. J. Savage, the popular Unitarian minister of Boston, in a sermon on the "Causes and Cure of Poverty," reported by the Boston Transcript in 1876, advised, first, compulsory education, second industrial training, and third, "*some means ought to be provided for checking the birth of sickly children.*" He also advised public sanitation and systematic charity.

In England, France and Italy there are many outspoken advocates of Neo-Malthusianism. A few of their names and quotations have already been given, and a few more follow.

Mr. Montague Cookson, Q. C., in an article which appeared in the Fortnightly Review of October, 1872, wrote: "It would be interesting if it were not melancholy to observe the way in which, both in writing and speaking, men are perpetually admitting the material inconveniences due to an excess of population, whilst they give the go-by to the obvious solution that the numbers of children born after marr age should be limited. * * * The limitation of the number of the family ought to be secured by obedience to natural laws which all may discover and verify if they will, and such limitation is as much the duty of married persons as the observance of chastity is the duty of those that are unmarried. One of the main wants of the day is, as I conceive, the formation of a sound public opinion on this subject."

Dr. Bertillon, writing upon the subject of "Marriage or Matrimonial Hygiene" in the Dictionnaire Encyclopedique Des Sciences Medicales," says:

"Here the ticklish question of moral or immoral restraint crops up. * * * * The object of which is not to procreate children, unless with the intention of so doing. This is a delicate problem that raises the anger of many. It might be objected that it is incomprehensible why man, who holds that it is wise, nay, obligatory, not to act without intention, and a foreknowledge of his acts, and who repudiates in everything thoughtless surrender to the instincts of passion, should reject a rule that he deems just when the most serious act that he can be called upon to perform comes in question—the procreation of a human being—an act, the consequence of which he will have to bear during the whole of his life."

Prof. Paola Mantegazza, Senator of Italy, professor of anthropology in Florence, one of the most eminent and popular writers of Italy, whose "Elements of Hygiene" has had six editions, has expressed himself thus: "In our eyes the problem as to the morality of the Malthusian reticences may be stated frankly in this way: When two human beings love each other, and yet from bad health of one or both of them there is every likelihood that diseased children will result from their marriage, is it a greater fault to beget epileptic, tuberculous or ricketty children, or to prevent fecundation? When from the excessive increase of the family itself human beings are brought into the world almost inexorably condemned to hunger, to degradation, to disease, is it a greater sin to limit the number of children or to increase the sufferings of the human family?"

In England during the past six years there has been a society called the Malthusian League, the objects of which are: "First, to agitate for the abolition of all penalties on the public discussion of the population question, and to obtain such a statutory definition as shall render it impossible in the future, to bring such discussions within the scope of the common law as a misdemeanor. Second, to spread among the people, by all practicable means, a knowledge of the law of population, of its consequences, and of its bearing upon human conduct and morals."

The president of this society is C. R. Drysdale, M.D., Lond. F.R.C.S., and among the vice-presidents are the names of the following eminent persons: Mr. C. Bradlaugh, M.P., Mrs. Annie Besant, M. Yves Guyot, of Paris, Senor Aldecoa, Director of Government Charities at Madrid, etc. There is a medical branch of the League in which are enlisted twenty-five physicians residing in various parts of Europe and Asia, and one of their objects is "To obtain a body of scientific opinion on points of sexual physiology and pathology involved in the population question, and which can only be discussed by those possessed of scientific knowledge."

Membership in the League requires a payment of two shillings annually, which entitles the subscriber to receive the Malthusian, the monthly organ of the society. All persons interested in this subject who may desire to aid the only organization yet established to effect its objects, as above stated, should communicate with its secretary, Mr. W. H. Reynolds, 63 Fleet St., E. C., London, England.

# CHAPTER V.

## WHY NOT

### Adopt Contraception as the Means to the End of Regulating Reproduction and Checking Reckless Propagation?

" Why Not " is the title of "A Book for Every Woman," by Dr. H. R. Storer, of Boston, issued as long ago as 1866, the object of which was to make plain to women the reasons *why* they should *not* resort to abortion. That it is well written for the purpose, is apparent to every reader, outside of the fact that it was awarded a gold medal by the American Medical Association, as a prize essay. Nothing is said on the subject of contraception, excepting in the preface to the second edition, in which he devotes six lines to say that "methods of prevention are uniformly injurious, and that, of them all, incomplete intercourse, by whatever way effected, is probably the worst." He avoids stating what "course should be pursued where there exists mental derangement, either in husband or wife," or other cause *why* children should *not* be procreated. I have already referred to the fact that this Neo-Malthusian idea or suggestion has met with opposition, even to the extent of criminal prosecution of its publishers, a fate not uncommon, however, to new scientific thought in any direction, if so be that it seriously clash with current religious or moral ideas, and in the medical world, also, there is a tenacity to old notions and a bigoted opposition to innovations which every reform affecting its domain is likely to feel. So, when we propose contraception as a ready method for solving the problem, what shall be done to check reckless propagation and to favor scientific breeding of the human race, and ask of it "why not?" we are favored with unfavorable replies on national, religious, moral and medical or physiological grounds.

So far as a nation is concerned, I think I have fairly shown that the doctrine of "fewer children and better," if applied, would favor a larger, healthier and thriftier adult population than results from the hap-hazard efforts to increase and multiply now in vogue. Under the new regime there would be less waste of life, health and wealth, less vice and misery, resulting from overcrowding, less of all those positive population checks which, in their operation of thinning out the ranks of coming generations, leave many of those who live through them in a crippled, diseased or demoralized condition, so that few, indeed, run the gauntlet unscathed.

So far as religion is concerned, the only organization having influence over the masses, as John Stuart Mill has said, is the Roman Catholic, which, if I mistake not, inculcates the idea that as many children should be procreated as possible, it mattering little if they die young, if only there be time to administer to them the rite of baptism. Accepting the dogma that Heaven welcomes them all, and that it is a good thing to be born under any circumstance, providing the priest be called at death, however early, it is difficult to frame an argument against the most utter abandonment to the business of begetting, though in the light of such a view it is also difficult for me to find a reason for, or justification of, celibacy.

Where, however, even the communicants of the Roman
Catholic Church become enlightened to their own self-
interest, the branding of "conjugal prudence" as a sin,
has not availed to abolish this custom.  In an appendix
to the report of the trial of Edward Truelove for publishing the Hon. Robert Dale Owen's Moral Physiology, may
be found quite a lengthy translation of a petition to the
Vatican Council, written originally in Latin in the year
1870 by a French priest, who announced himself humbly
to be "a thoroughly devoted son of the Holy Catholic
Apostolic Roman Church."   It is a very remarkable petition, which we should like to quote entire, but instead
will endeavor to select the main points, as follows:

### Argument of a Liberal Priest.

"Natural morality requires married persons suffering
from any transmissable disease to abstain from propa-
gating it in the world by giving themselves a wretched
posterity; but the desires of these married persons
remain, although to the morality of nature which cries,
'If you cannot contain, at least shun the procreation of
miserable and mischievous beings,' the scholastic morality replies: 'Absolute abstentation or procreation, to
the bitter end ; no middle course!'  Between the two
precepts the opposition is formal (positive, complete)
Which morality is the purest—that is, the truest: The
morality that scholasticism has inscribed in books, or
the morality that God has inscribed on the hearts of
men?  It will be our duty to search in the holy books
alone for the condemnation of the act in question; if it
be not found to be forbidden by the decalogue, nor by
the other laws of God found in Holy Writ, nor by the
Apostles, nor by the commands of the Church assembled
in Council-general, nor by the Pope speaking *ex-cathedra*,
we shall say it cannot be condemned by anybody.  If
the Church had ever pronounced formally against this

practice that we are discussing—and that is not the case
we should entreat her not to repudiate this pronounced
decision, although it would be out of harmony with the
march of humanity, but at least to shut her eyes; for she
will be impotent to curb it. We know, and every one is
acquainted with, examples of good and zealous christians
in every respect, except that they cannot come to the
sacraments because they are unable to obey their confessors on this head. We have desired to demonstrate
that the act is condemned on impressions, not as the
result of serious examination. We have proved that it
does not constitute a murder; that the sacrament of marriage is not harmed in the least by it; that after having
rejected it, following the lead of the theologians,
philosophy is forced to admit it as necessary; that it is
not forbidden in a single line of a single holy book; that
generation is not the sole end of marriage, and that the
pacification of the flesh, which is another end, ought to
find its place; that in our time, certain laws, made for
the epoch of Noah, are not only inapplicable, but some
would be criminal. It is not the sin that is new, but the
circumstances that have changed. This practice has
spread more in the last half century by the force of
events. *Other times, other manners; laws ought to follow
manners.* The confessors, when driven, little by little,
into a corner, not wishing to put themselves in opposition either to their judgment, which shows them the
truth, or to their authors, who bind them, permit and
go so far as to *advise* means of lessening the chances of
conception; the choice of the period when it is held to
be impossible. A learned and religious devotee of a
very austere Order, says: 'I have studied this case with
all the powers of my intelligence and of my conscience,
and I have come to this formal conviction, that we are
on the wrong track. To my mind, this act is enormously
below the smallest mortal sin, and it is again enormously

lessened by all the motives that provoke it—real motives of health, even of interest, of family, etc.' Others having studied the question thoroughly, have acknowledged that they were bound by an error of modern theology; and they solicit that it be redressed. They understand that this movement cannot be arrested by rules and regulations, because it is in the logic of things, because it is necessary. Also they ardently solicit a decision in harmony with the necessities of the time, and they practice, meanwhile, all the tolerance that their conscience is able to permit."

### Physiological and Moral Objections.

Next let us consider the physiological and moral objections to contraception, and on this field the skirmish (for it is hardly a close battle as yet), is at present, and has been for some time, a triangular contest between three parties:

1st. Those arrayed under the flag of the Alpha, declaring for celibacy before marriage, and "marital continence" in marriage, with no exception "except for purpose of reproduction."

2nd. Those who admit that under some circumstances (with a large variety of opinion with reference to the circumstances) it is proper, wise and expedient to advise or make use of contraceptics, but that they should not be generally accessible.

3rd. Those who believe that the science and art of contraception should be studied, developed and improved, and that what is now known or hereafter to be discovered should be published, as is all science, without fear or favor.

Doing battle, as I shall, from the third standpoint, let me level my guns first upon the small but sturdy guard of the Alpha flag, not with any expectation of routing them, or any desire to spike their guns, for we agree with them in some points as thoroughly as we disagree in others, and our battle with them is mainly to maintain our own position and show that we are right in holding it. The first party claim to hold the most advanced ground "founded upon religion, science and the highest and purest morality and philanthropy," and into the camp of the third party they throw this hot shot, viz.: That any exercise of the sexual function except for procreation, is "immoral, unnatural and injurious." This the third party repels and denies, while loading and firing in return the historical fact that the most strenuous religious, moral and governmental efforts to enforce celibacy and continence have been not only unsuccessful, but inevitably and proportionately attended with physical degeneracy and moral debasement, and notably with an increase of prostitution. The war of words and ideas between these two parties, and the available amunition, are exhibited in a pamphlet entitled "Dr. Foote's Replies to the Alphites," a war, by the way, with which both parties seem to be satisfied, since each believes that "our side came off victorious."

Being myself well satisfied that the third party has in this discussion well held its ground, I will not review the entire field, but merely add a few fortifications.

### Contraception as a Moral Question.

As to the morality or immorality of contraception, it depends largely upon personal bias or preference, and upon one's general philosophy of life. If man has been placed upon earth, or finds himself here merely for the purpose of multiplying and giving place to his successors, then this must be the sole use and function of the sexual organs, and the more they are devoted to it the better, till the earth shall be replenished to its fullest capacity, but if we may believe that "as we journey through life" it is moral and proper that we

"live by the way," may we not attribute to this function
a duplex utility,* as we do to the sense of taste of which
no one denies us the enjoyment, though its main purpose and use is evidently to guide in the selection of
food; or, the sense of hearing since, to the sounds approaching our ears, we do not say "no admittance
except on business," for we are glad also to receive those
which contribute only to our pleasure—as in listening
to music. The morality of an act is also to be judged
by its results, and if it be shown to contribute to the
happiness and well-being of mankind without impair-
ing physical or mental integrity, it may be accepted as
good; and again, morality is to be considered relatively,
and an act may be taken as moral or immoral, according
as good or evil predominates in it.† Therefore, were it
true, as claimed by ultra-moralists that there ought, in
the perfect state, to be no indulgence of the sexual passion except for procreation, and that only under such
conditions as would favor the best quality of offspring,

* The Rev. H. W. Marsh, in his work, "Science and the Bible,"
speaking of the dual sexual nature of humanity, writes : "The end
and object of this arrangement was not only the multiplication of
the species, but also the enhancement of happiness to each, by the
interchange of those amiable affections, and those offices of
sympathy and kindness which should arise from the inherent
diversity of character in the sexes."

†"We emphatically deny that sexual intercourse, without results,
does constitute vice, or is immoral. Even the 'Holy Sacrament
of Marriage,' according to the established Church, appears to
recognize this, for it provides for the sexual union of persons
necessarily sterile, and omits certain prayers when the woman is
past child-bearing. Even to the most obtuse understanding it is
obvious that ninety per cent., at least, of the sexual intercourse of
married persons bears no possible relation to the reproduction of
the species. To the rational understanding, vice can only be constituted by any action, or abstinence from action, the ultimate
outcome of which is a withdrawal or defection from the happiness
of the individual or of the society greater than its addition thereto;
and virtue by that which tends to increase or establish harmony
between the organism and its environment."—E. Persey P. Mac.
Loghlin, M.R.C.S., in the Provincial Medical Journal, October
1, 1885.

it is at once apparent that this standard is so far beyond the existing practice and belief that it can be adopted in but comparatively rare instances as a working formula, and while we are awaiting the approach of the millennial day when it will be universally welcomed, we might avail ourselves of something a little less divine and perfect, by which to give humanity a lift out of the present slough of imperfection. For the present and some centuries to come, we may as well depend upon contraception as a lesser evil to help us up toward the greater good, if so it be, of strict continence. ‡

## The Sexual Status To-Day.

To appreciate how far society, as a whole, is from being ready to accept the Alphite theory, let us inquire what is the status of public opinion on sexual affairs. It was brought out by the late "exposure" of sexual vice

---

‡ "I Deny the position of the Shaker, then, that the instinct is justifiable (if, indeed, it be at all), only as necessary to the reproduction of the species. It is justifiable, in my view, just in as far as it makes man a happier and a better being. It is justifiable, both as a source of temperate enjoyment, and as a means by which the sexes can mutually polish and improve each other. I found all my arguments on the position that the pleasure derived from this instinct, independent of and totally distinct from its ultimate object, the reproduction of the race, is good, proper, worth securing and enjoying, I maintain that its temperate enjoyment is a blessing, both in itself and in its influence on human character." —From *Robert Dale Owen's* "*Moral Physiology.*"

"Some argue that with a beloved wife beside him, the man should either pass his life in struggling against a legitimate passion, the pacification of which is necessary to him, or that whatever his situation should be, he should be forced to oppress himself with heavy responsibilities dangerous to himself and society! It would be absolutely forbidden him to seek a middle term between the two extremes of this impossible dilemma. This prohibition, contrary to nature, to reason, to the interests of humanity, none but the maker of man himself has a right to lay down as a rule. And here we are in strictness. If God has not pronounced it in formal terms, nobody can seek it out by induction or by supposition. Where is this absolute, formal prohibition to be found in writing?"—*From a French priest's petition to the Vatican Council.*

in London by the Pall Mall Gazette.    It is not necessary
here to cite the facts discovered and published concerning the systematic pursuit of vice (involving actual
crimes) by some aristocrats, titled personages, etc., the
truth of which has been attested, after due examination,
by eminent churchmen and statesmen.    Perhaps the
most remarkable fact developed by this "great sensation" was that the good people who were so horrified by
it, those who at once became clamorous for reform in
legislation, merely demanded that the age at which a
girl should be privileged to give her consent to "illicit
intercourse" should be made sixteen or eighteen instead
of thirteen, as it then was, while it was actually em-
bodied in the petition for reform that no request
would be made that the actions of adults in such affairs
should be under legal restraint.    So it stands in England
that fornication is no criminal offence, and to judge by
other recent developments, it is not a sin in the eyes of
society so long as no voluntary or accidental exposure
makes a public scandal of a private relationship.    So it
is in New York State to-day, where even adultery is no
offence, against the law, and where, according to the
view of a judge now on the bench, it would be far less
practicable to enact, enforce and find jail-room for the
offenders against a law prohibitory of fornication,
adultery and prostitution, than to enact and make a
success of a prohibitory liquor law.    In a late political
campaign our attention was frequently called to another
straw indicating the direction of public sentiment—an
editorial in the New York Evening Post, a "highly
moral and respectable family journal," stating, as though
it were universal, the opinion that "chastity is a great
virtue, but every man knows in his heart that it is not
the greatest of virtues, that offences against it have often
been consistent with the possession of *all* the qualities
which ennoble human life and make progress possible."

It is fair to state, on the other hand, that another New York daily, the Tribune, often used this quotation against the Post, assuming superior virtue.

In the memoirs of Caroline Bauer, the Morganatic wife of Prince Leopold, she gives amusing and interesting reminiscences of life as she saw it in the city of St. Petersburg fifty years ago. She had letters of introduction to the pastor of the German congregation there, Rev. Johannes Muralt, whom she found to be living openly with the Countess Fersen "upon a footing which only fell short of marriage through an omission of the ceremony," and the congregation "saw nothing objectionable in the domestic arrangements of their shepherd; his great virtues lovingly covered his little weaknesses." The pastor's own excuse for not inviting the ceremony was simply and plainly that he was too fond of his personal liberty, or to use his own words, "I cannot make up my mind to marry because I want to remain free and keep myself in a position that I can pack up at any time. The enjoyment of domestic life I possess in full measure in the manner of living which I arranged twelve years ago. I feel merrier and happier than any pater-familias."

What clergymen and others then did openly, they must now do secretly in order to maintain their position and standing; a difference, to be sure, but how great the improvement? is another question, for, that men standing eminently before the public, clerically, professionally and politically, *may* retain their popularity because of "great virtues," even though it is generally believed or tacitly understood that they are prone to such "little weaknesses" as was Herr Muralt, has been proven in numerous instances during the past ten years. There would appear to be a sort of unwritten and unspoken but tacitly implied moral law that a man may enjoy his "personal liberty" in the way so dear to the heart of

Herr Muralt, so long as he so carefully minds his own business that his private affairs shall not become public affairs. A noted English liberal summoned as correspondent in a suit for divorce, will, says the keen-sighted correspondent of the New York Tribune, suffer little or no loss of popularity should he succeed in escaping a court conviction, although the facts against him are already sufficiently evident to the ordinary mind.

Again, the Utah Commission has made its annual report to the United States Government, renewing past recommendations and submitting additional ones, one of which is, "That all persons be excluded by law from making a location or settlement upon any part of the lands of the United States who shall refuse on demand to take an oath * * * that he does not cohabit with *more than one woman in the marriage relation*," etc. When this commission takes pains, as it does by the use of extra words, to make an exception of the man living with more than one woman *in the marriage relation*, does it not appear that the latest governmental position on the question of sexual morality is that bigamy or polygamy is an offense while concubinage is not? Indeed, this philosophy is already to be found in Anti-Mormon laws, and if the new recommendation of the commission should be adopted it would only be a re-statement of it in a new form. When the anti-polygamy law was passed in the shape it now stands, inculpating the polygamist and excepting the man of many concubines, there was but one voice, that of Senator Brown, of Georgia, raised against the method of it, and one voice prevails not against a multitude.

Until the Alphites shall have educated the people to the "higher standard" to that extent that they will voluntarily render allegiance to the rule of continence out of marriage, or at least convince enough of them to make possible the enactment of a law making fornication and

adultery an offence, it is not likely that they will achieve
any considerable success in reforming humanity through
the advocacy of "marital continence." Prof. Frederick
Henry Gerrish, of the Portland (Maine) Medical School,
in an address before the Maine Medical Association at
its annual meeting in 1878, on "The Duties of the Medical Profession concerning Prostitution and its Allied
Vices," suggests first among remedial means the enforcement of existing laws against fornication, adultery and
indecency, but at once admits "it is plain that vice will
always exist." He says:

"We have very few trials in the courts for adultery,
but the crime is committed thousands of times every
year; fornication is almost never made a matter of indictment, though it is one of the commonest of offences.
There is law enough about them already" (which may be
taken either way, "as you like it;") "all that is needed
is a public sentiment to uphold the officers in executing
its prosecution." If the officials would first convict
themselves and take up their abode behind the bars, the
unofficial offenders might experience a change of heart
and follow them in without the expense of public trial.
I offer this as a substitute for Dr. Gerrish's motion, but
as he remarks of one of his better propositions, "the
most sanguine must admit that it will be some generations before even the small portion of the world, which
we call civilized, will be sufficiently educated to adopt
such suggestions." Some of us, un-Pharisaical common
folks, cannot help wondering whether these ultra-
moralists, when not superannuated, semi-paralyzed or
biting sour grapes, religiously practice what they preach.

### Mr. Hypocritical Artful-Dodger, M.D.

In London, following close upon the sensation or
excitement occasioned by the prosecution of Mr. Bradlaugh and Mrs. Besant for selling Dr. Knowlton's

"Fruits of Philosophy," which caused the sale of nearly
two hundred thousand copies of that book, there was
held in August of 1877 a meeting of the Obstetrical Section of the British Medical Association, at which Mr. C.
H. F. Routh, M. D., M.R.C.P., etc., etc., was requested
to open this subject of Neo-Malthusianism for the discussion of the society.    This was subsequently published
in pamphlet form in the preface to which Dr. Routh
refers to "a disreputable work which had been largely
circulated," and he felicitates himself upon the boldness
with which he came forward "on so indecorous a subject," persuaded, however, for the sake of "the public
good;" while in return for the vote of thanks from the
members of the section, he acknowledges "their manly
Christian deportment and their bold example," which he
trusts "will destroy this many-headed monster from the
realm."    This is a high-toned and forcible beginning,
and when, in the body of his address, we find artificial
means to prevent fructification denominated "sexual
fraudulency," and described as "a base and moral
crime, against which the whole body of the medical profession should protest," we begin to feel that here is a
genuine, earnest, uncompromising Alphite; and we become more confirmed in this faith in reading "there is
such a thing as moral restraint," "greater is the man
that ruleth his spirit than he that taketh a city," "let
the passions be kept down by athletics, hard mental
work and industrial occupations," etc.; but read a little
further, and read back again to analyze more closely his
meaning, and we discover that the main power of his
invective and argument has been directed against one
special, and perhaps the most objectionable method of
contraception, and against excess rather than moderation
of indulgence; and lastly, we find him actually suggest-
ing a means of indulgence which may be unfruitful, for
to the married who for good cause should avoid child-

bearing, he says, "*methodize your conjugal relations*," and citing Mayer's "twelve-day rule"* he admits "within these physiological limits it may be wise to regulate restraint, if not imperative wholly to practice it, but let it not be made an excuse or a cloak for fraudulency." This writer and the gentlemen who, in the discussion following, complimented him upon handling the subject "so moderately and chastely as to prevent any possible misconstruction on the part of any person of ordinary intelligence," did in fact dodge and talk round the subject after the manner of all hypocrites, so that it is really difficult for a person of ordinary intelligence to learn accurately what their opinions are in detail, but it is evident enough that Dr. Routh and his eminent coadjutors, while assuming a lofty attitude of superiority to the common herd of Neo-Malthusian philosophers and hurling "abhorrence and disgust" at them, have practically themselves *let down the bars*, and opened the way for any and every physiologically harmless contraceptic. But Dr. Routh has not only dropped thus far from the high moral standard of the Alphites; he has said,[1] "let the mothers do their duty by their children, and suckle them as they are bound to do, and so they shall not procreate more frequently than is consistent with health;" which is to suggest and approve the practice of extending lactation to avoid conception, and that is as "abominable" as the other methods he abhors; for these reasons:—

It is depleting and otherwise injurious to the mother.

* What is familiarly known as the twelve, fourteen or fifteen-day rule, or the supposition that there is a period of infertility of about one week, beginning fourteen days after menstruation, involves the further supposition that the ripened ovule passes away about this time, and that the next one is not ready for impregnation until a few days before the next menstruation. It is far from being invariably or generally reliable, and there is no way to determine when or by whom it can be relied upon.

It impedes development and impairs the health of the nursling.

It is not a reliable method of contraception, and therefore there may be a second child (in utero) to suffer mal-nutrition.

Thus Dr. Routh couragiously assaults one ill-advised method of contraception only to propose an equally bad one, and the best he has to offer does not meet the requirements in being entirely reliable and harmless; but mark the monstrous inconsistency and exhibition of hypocrisy on the part of this gilt-edged, goody-good medical man in quoting, as he does, without criticism and in the line of his argument the silly statement that "a choked germ rendered unproductive is an indirect infanticide," and then concluding his paper with information regarding an interval or period of time when "connection is not likely to lead to impregnation"— when of necessity all seed sown is upon sterile ground, and every one becomes a "choked germ rendered unproductive." A man so befuddled in his reason can hardly be regarded as an expert on physiological morals or a reliable judge of any question. The real trouble with such men is that they are on the fence, "neither this nor that," and they make a botch of it when trying to use words to conceal thoughts.

### Is Contraception "Unnatural" and Therefore Evil?

The above reference to germs rendered unproductive is part of the charge that any interference with their productivity is "unnatural"—"a violation of nature's laws, and a frustration of nature's ends." To this Mrs. Besant has well replied :—

"To limit the family is no more a violation of nature's laws than to preserve the sick by medical skill; the restriction of the birth-rate does not violate nature's laws more than does the restriction of the death-rate. Science

strives to diminish the positive checks; science should
also discover the best preventive checks. We only teach
conjugal prudence by balancing one natural force against
another. Such study of nature, and such balancing of
natural forces, is civilization. The human brain is
nature's highest product, and all improvements on irrational nature are most purely natural; preventive checks
are no more unnatural than every other custom of civilization. Raw meat, nakedness, living in caves, these are
the *irrational* natural habits; cooked food, clothes,
houses, these are the *rational* natural customs. Production of offspring recklessly, carelessly, lustfully, this is
irrational nature, and every brute can here outdo us;
production of offspring with forethought, earnestness,
providence, this is rational nature, where man stands
alone."

The unproductive germs are indeed wasted, but this
is to some extent, at least, an inevitable waste. Here is
needed an explanation regarding waste. Nature knows
nothing of it. All matter is grist in her mill and is
utilized in some form or other. Pollen, wafted by the
wind, may or may not be the means of fructification, but
the vast amount of it which is not utilized in its highest
capacity may serve as food for animal life, or merely as
manure for sprouting plants. The word waste is an in-
vention of man—a little idea of his own. Nature keeps
no account and makes no complaint of the waste of
human life in what we look upon as terrible infant mortality. Cold mother earth accepts the remains, and so
much substance committed to her laboratory to be trans-
formed and worked over again into living forms. Only
man has reason to bemoan the loss or waste which I have
shown to be so prodigious, of fructified germs of human
beings, and from the human and humane point of view
I protest against this sort of waste, and propose that the
inevitable waste shall be restricted to the domain of un-

fertilized germs; or, in other words, the waste should be kept as far as possible on the contraceptic side of the line, rather than allowed to invade, so largely as it does now, the abortive side. It is, in fact, just as moral and natural (and often more wise) to keep the two seeds apart, as it is to keep the sexes apart.

According to the moral and religious creeds of one hundred and sixty millions of people of India, the keeping of the sexes apart, after the fruitful period is reached, is a crime. In the institutes of Narada, which may be regarded as the Hindoo Bible and law book, there is this sentence in reference to the duty of procreation: "No girl should let the period of maturity come on without giving notice to her relatives; if they thereupon do not give her in marriage to a husband, they are similar to *murderers of embryos.*" Here is the ancient origin of the idea that "a choked germ rendered unproductive is an indirect infanticide," and those who propose to stand by that assertion should have the consistency of the Hindoos, and adopt their uncompromising rules in reference to early marriage. A compendium of Hindoo law gives this warning: "A girl, before her breasts are prominent, should be given in marriage, and he who delays such marriage shall sink to a region of torment." Behold the logic of the anti-preventionists, carried to its ultimatum; are they ready to say amen?

Dr. Alexander Wilder, in the article already once quoted from in an earlier chapter, further says:

"What the exact standard of morality in this matter should be, we acknowledge is not easy to ascertain, as would at first seem. Theologians meet the question glibly enough, but physiologists have the real difficulties to encounter. In the course of nature, in all departments of organic existence, there are a thousand ways provided for semination, where one instance occurs of actual procreation. In every animal are the germs, ova

and other agents for abundant fecundation; yet most of
them fall short, or the world would be speedily over-run.
The same analogy holds good with the human race.
Every woman has the capacity for producing twenty or
more children, and by the logic which inhibits the preventing of conception, ought to have them. Yet, so
many births might overcrowd the world, and become an
evil and a calamity. Besides, if married women have no
moral right to avoid maternity, parity of reasoning
would enforce the same doctrine on the unmarried.
Their capacities and aptitudes are similar, and they
suffer as 'much or more by the avoidance. Among the
animal races, all females are privileged alike, and physiology has not yet ascertained why such women should
constitute an exception. Yet moralists inculcate a wholesale waste of their sexual functions."

During thirty years of the life of every unmarried
woman who lives to the age of forty-five, there occurs
thirteen times in each year, or nearly six hundred times
altogether, the extrusion of an ovule which required only
the fecundating influence, at the proper time, to constitute it the inception and abode of human life; and each
of the two ovaries is made up of many thousand cells,
each one of which stands ready, should opportunity
offer, to blossom into an ovule and invite impregnation.
Of the male element, the sperm-cells, it may be said that
for every one which effects its true physiological function (fecundation), millions of them must, of necessity,
fail to be of service. The waste, as we might as well call
it, in the unfertilized seed, is simply inestimable, and
being part of nature's method of procreation, must continue till all life ceases, but this need not in the least
lessen the comforts or happiness of mankind, so long as
it be not permitted to be *unphysiologically excessive;* but
the waste of fecundated ova in abortions and premature
deaths is attended with numerous individual misfor-

tunes and social evils, which it is our duty to prevent so far as we may be able to do so by the application of scientific methods in all departments of life, including contraception as the radical remedy against super-fecundity.

## Is Contraception Physically Injurious?

To make any satisfactory reply to the Alphites upon this important question, it would be necessary to go minutely into the discussion of ways and means, to compare freely the various methods of contraception which have been adopted or proposed, and to carefully weigh all the objections offered on physiological grounds against these several methods; but not being ready to enter upon this practical department of the subject, we will be content here with merely stating the opinion of many competent physicians who have had good opportunities for studying the merits and demerits of many contraceptic methods, viz.: The opinion that while there are more bad than good ones, yet there are means which are entitled to be considered as fairly reliable and harmless--in fact, physiologically unobjectionable.

## Comstock, Colgate & Co. (Limited).

Having given sufficient attention to the Alphites, for present purposes, I pass on to a consideration of the position of the second party, those who recognize the utility of contraceptics, while at the same time assuming to discover in them a dangerous element which makes it seem to them wise and expedient to hedge them about with prohibitory laws; laws which were enacted by their request, and whose enforcement has thus far been left to their judgment or discretion, if we can really attribute such qualities to them. The sentiment which regards contraceptics as articles to be suppressed, took an organized form about the year 1870, becoming incorporated under the title of the "Society for the Suppression of Vice," but since the prime movers and active members of the concern were less than a dozen busy-bodies who took upon themselves the task of directing and regulating the morals of the rest of the many millions of inhabitants of the United States, they may as well be called, as they are generally known, as Comstock, Colgate & Co. (Limited); and the word "limited" may, in this instance, be understood to cover a multitude of sins, for they are limited in numbers, in fact a close corporation, limited in general intelligence, gumption and common sense, limited in faith, hope and charity for the human race, and limited (judging from their own annual plaints and complaints) in their purse and power to suppress everything which doesn't exactly harmonize with their narrow and limited philosophy of morals. They succeeded, however, in moving congress and several State legislatures to enact new laws in reference to obscene literature and immoral articles, in which they incorporated clauses constituting contraceptics contraband, and making it a misdemeanor to manufacture, sell, give away or possess any article or thing designed or intended for the prevention of conception. In a recent trial in New York City, of a man charged with having offended against this portion of the penal code, the Judge, in his charge to the jury, gave them to understand that the object of this legislation was to prevent checking increase of population. He quoted from some jurist a paragraph showing how the prosperity and wealth of a nation was largely dependent upon population, and the judge evidently believed that it was from some consideration of that kind that the legislature had been prevailed upon to enact the law, but he was, we feel quite sure, entirely mistaken in that opinion. The argument which has been relied upon to move legislatures in this matter, is simply this, as Mrs. Besant puts it: "That the knowledge of these scientific checks would make vice bolder, and would increase unchastity among women by making it safe." Let us follow her terse statement of this objection to contraceptics by her reply to it:

"Suppose that this were so, it might save some broken hearts and some deserted children; men ruin women and go scatheless, and then bitterly object that their victims escape something of public shame. And if so, are all to suffer, so that one or two, already corrupt in heart, may be preserved from becoming corrupt in act? Are mothers to die slowly, that impure women may be held back, and wives to be sacrificed, that the unchaste may be curbed? As well say that no knives must be used because throats may be cut with them; no matches sold because incendiarism may result from them; no pistols allowed because murders may be committed by them. Blank ignorance has some advantages in the way of safety, and if all men's eyes were put out, none would ever be tempted to seduce a woman for her beauty. Let us bring for our women the veil to cover, and the eunuch to guard, and so be at least consistent in our folly and our distrust! But this knowledge would *not* increase unchastity; the women who could thus use it would be solely those who only lack opportunity, not will, to go astray: the means suggested all imply deliberation and forethought; are these generally the handmaids of un-chastity? English women are not yet sunk so low that they preserve their loyalty to one, only from fear of the possible consequences of disloyalty; their purity, their pride, their honor, their womanhood, these are the guardians of their virtue, and never from English women's heart will fade the maiden and matronly dig-nity, which makes them shield their love from all taint of impurity, and bid them only surrender themselves, where the surrender of the heart and of pledged faith have led the way. Shame on those who slander England's wives and maidens with the foul thoughts that can only spring from the mind and the lips of the profligate."

Another argument in reply to those who assert that contraceptics favor vice, is found in "The Fruits of Philosophy," by Charles Knowlton, M.D., an American (Mass.) physician of fifty years ago. It is part of the appendix of that pamphlet, and reads as follows:

"The only seeming objection of much weight that can be brought against diffusing a knowledge of checks is, that it will serve to increase illegal connections. Now this is exactly the contrary effect of that which those who have diffused such knowledge most confidently believe will arise from it. To diminish such connections is indeed one of the grand objects of these publications—an object which laws and prisons cannot, or at least do not, accomplish. Why is there so much prostitution in the land? The true answer to the question is not, and never will be—because the people have become acquainted with certain facts in physiology. It is because there are so many unmarried men and women—men of dissipation and profligacy, owing to their not having married in their younger days and settled down in life. But why are there so many unmarried people in the country? Not because young hearts, when they arrive at the age of maturity, do not desire to marry, but because prudential considerations interfere. The young man thinks I cannot marry yet, I cannot support a family, I must make money first, and think of a matrimonial settlement afterwards. And so it is that, through fear of having a family, before they have made a little head-way in the world, and of being thereby compelled to 'tug at the oar of incessant labor throughout their lives,' thousands of young men do not marry, but go abroad into the world, and form vicious acquaintances and practices. The truth, then, is this, there is so much

of illegal connection in the land, because the people had
not, twenty years ago, that very information which, it
would seem, to some, doubtless through want of due
reflection, are apprehensive will increase this evil. I
might quote pages to the point from 'Every Woman's
Book;' but I fear my communication would be too
lengthy. I content myself with a few lines. 'But when
it has become the custom here as elsewhere to limit the
number of children, so that none need have more than
they wish, no man will fear to take a wife; all will marry
while young; debauchery will diminish; while good
morals and religious duties will be promoted.'"

### Abortion Lawful—Contraception Criminal.

One would naturally suppose that an association of
men who should urge and put through laws shutting
down entirely on the manufacture and sale of contraceptics, must be thoroughly convinced that there could
be no legitimate use for them, or, that having what
might be called a compromise opinion in regard to them,
that they would have included in their framing of a new
law some excepting clause which would have made it
possible for them to be sold under certain restrictions,
as for instance by the advice or prescription of a physician; but they did not have sense or sagacity enough for
that, and as the laws now stand in any case where a
married woman cannot safely become a mother, it is not
possible for a physician *legally* to supply or direct means
of prevention of conception, though *it is lawful*, should
conception occur, for him *to produce abortion* to insure
the mother's life, or rather to relieve her from the danger
of a birth at full term. Behold, then, the result of laws
based upon so-called moral sentiments instead of scientific reasoning; whereby prevention of conception is
constituted an offence when abortion is not. Therefore
if the laws were obeyed, the practical result would be a

great number of abortions where contraception might serve instead; but the fact is that physicians and laymen take liberties with the law, and where it becomes a necessity to decide between lawful abortion and unlawful contraception, they prefer to break the man-made law against contraceptics rather than the natural law against abortion.   It has therefore come about that one of the least well observed laws of the State is that applying to contraceptics, a fact well known to Comstock, Colgate & Co., who wink at infractions of it by themselves and many others, but use it as often as they choose and as opportunity affords for the persecution of their enemies, or for the purpose of making a raid* when there is nothing else handy to attack in their line, and it is deemed necessary to make a show of activity.   We take this opportunity to make one more protest against a law which is not congenial to the thoughts, wishes or habits of the people to whom it applies, and which, under the circumstances may be so readily made use of for malicious or black-mailing purposes.

### President Colgate's Vaseline Contraceptic.

Having attributed to Comstock, Colgate & Co., the holding of the opinion that contraceptics have their useful and proper field of employment, it is only fair that the reasons for so doing should be given.   The first evidence we have to offer is a matter of history that has been often enough told, but is essential to this place. Within about five years of the time when Mr. Samuel Colgate busied himself, with other members of the Co.,

---

* Such a raid was made in the fall of 1885, upon half a dozen of the hundreds of druggists in New York who were selling closed ring-pessaries.  Following the prophecy "one shall be taken and the other left, one prominent Broadway druggist was arrested while another equally *Hazard*-ous was not, but this was not so surprising, after all, when the name of the latter was found to appear on the subscription list of the Vice Society, while the former did not.

to obtain the passage of the law which forbids the mailing of any papers or advertisements in articles *designed* for the prevention of conception, he being appointed general agent for the sale of vaseline, and being desirous of extending the knowledge of its merits and uses, began mailing to the physicians of the United States a twelve-page pamphlet composed of some letters written by Dr. Henry A. DuBois, of San Rafael, Cal.  Among many other uses which this progressive physician had discovered for vaseline, was the following, as described in his own words on page 7 of Mr. Colgate's vaseline advertising pamphlet: "There is one use for this ointment that I have not fully worked out.  Physicians are frequently applied to to produce abortion.  Recently, on the same day, two women came to me; the reason assigned in the one case was that the husband was syphilitic; in the other, that pregnancy brought on violent attacks of spasmodic asthma.  Of course I explained that the child had rights as well as the mother, but it was all that I could do to prevent one of these cases from going to a professed abortionist.  In some cases of this kind prevention is better than cure, and I am inclined to think, from some experiments, that vaseline, charged with four to five grains of  *  *  *  *  acid,* will destroy spermatozoa, without injury to the uterus or vagina."

It is still a matter of question whether the mailing of this publication was or was not an infraction of the very mail law which Mr. Colgate was instrumental in having put on the statute books, but from the fact that evidence was offered to prove the mailing of a copy of the pam-

* The name of the acid is purposely omitted lest the publication of this prescription in full should place this page within the strict letter of the postal law, and constitute an offense which would not be as leniently dealt with as was Mr. Colgate's!  We are the more reconciled to this omission because, in our opinion, the use of strong solutions or ointments of such chemicals as **carbolic acid**, sulphate of zinc and sugar of lead, are, through continued use, injurious to the membranes of the parts.

phlet, which evidence, in the form of an affidavit, filed in the clerk's office of the U. S. Circuit Court of the Southern District of New York, together with the pamphlet itself in its original envelope, was not followed with indictment or prosecution—these facts go to show that if Mr. Colgate's pamphlet was not subject to the law, it certainly was a very clever evasion of it, for the prescription given was evidently *designed* for prevention of conception. If he had gone one step farther and offered to furnish the vaseline and acid in combination, put up in neat little bottles, with a label directing how to employ it for prevention of conception, the district attorney would hardly have dared to dismiss the case. But there can be no question that the issuing of this pamphlet in the manner described, put Mr. Colgate on record as one of that party or class of people who, as previously remarked, "admit that under some circumstances (with a large variety of opinion with reference to the circumstances), it is proper, wise and expedient to advise or make use of contraceptics, but that they should not be generally accessible." One great objection to the position taken by Colgate & Co., and all others of similar views, is that, in judging of the circumstances when it may be considered proper to advise or employ contraceptics, they are too apt to be biased in favor of themselves and their particular friends, and prejudiced against permitting similar liberties to those for whom they have no friendly interest. If it had so happened that the vaseline pamphlet had been issued by some other firm than that of Colgate & Co., the probabilities are that there would have been a great clamor about the U. S. Court by agents of the Vice Society, urging prosecution. It is only another instance of "whose ox was gored." It also seems appropriate to mention here that another person instrumental in the enactment of the Comstock postal law found the shoe to pinch himself

unpleasantly and sought relief.  It was a member of the
United States Congress who voted for the bill, thus
doing what he could to make a law of it, and before his
term expired applied to us in person for such articles as
he had voted to suppress.  It seemed hard to disappoint
so unselfish a friend of humanity, one who was so atten-
tive in looking after the morals of other folks that he
forgot his own (that is to say, his own needs), but he
went away not only without what he came for, but also
without something else he richly deserved—a dislocated
coccyx.

### Unfair and Unlawful Partiality.

To show that Comstock's opinion is in harmony with
that of his superior, it is only necessary to cite what he
said in reply to a physician in good practice in New York
City, who devised a peculiar form of pessary for which
he claimed many advantages and uses, one of which was
the prevention of conception, and who made inquiry of
the agent of the Vice Society whether there was anything
objectionable in his circular.  The reply was that the
form of circular making known the use of the pessary as
a contraceptic, was not permissible under the law, but
without the paragraph referring to this use of it, the
article and the circular were unobjectionable.  The fact
that it might be employed for the unlawful purpose, and
that its form and description would at once suggest the
possibility of such use for it, were not sufficient in themselves to cause the Vice Society to take cognizance of it
to interfere with its sale.  It was furthermore intimated
that the society had no desire to disturb regular physicians in advising such expedients as they might deem
advantageous to their patients, even these unlawful
ones; which being interpreted means that the old-school,
so-called "regular" physicians may do with this law as
they do with that against unlawful abortions, observe it

as much or as little as they please, without fear of suffering prosecution; the practical enforcement of such laws
being intended only for those who adopt a progressive
and independent position outside of the gilt-edged circle
of medical trades-unions. Another fact in reference to
this matter is that the Vice Society has no right to offer
immunity to any class of citizens, and in neglecting to
prosecute all impartially, even to the president of their
own society, they declare their unfitness for the work for
which the society was incorporated, viz.: the enforcement of the law as it stands. The incorporation of these
special societies for the suppression of vice and crime, is
in itself sufficiently un-American and undemocratic to
justify the large amount of opposition which is felt
toward them, but for such a society to request a certain
form of law as a tool to work with, ostensibly for the
benefit of morals, and then to apply it or not, according
to the whims, prejudices, and perhaps the private ends
of the executive officers, is an abuse of legislative power
which ought to be no longer permitted.

### Four Classes Affected by Laws Against Contraception.

Let us analyze the operation of these laws directed
against contraceptics. They affect four classes of the
community. (1) Physicians, Neo-Malthusians and those
moral philosophers who seek the improvement of the
human race through regulating reproduction by controlling conception; (2) those married persons who, for
reasons sufficient to themselves, desire to limit their
increase; (3) the criminal, vagrant and pauper classes,
including those whom Comstock and his aids speak
familiarly of as "crooked women;" (4) those young unmarried persons for whose especial protection and benefit the laws were enacted. The effect upon the first class
has been to discourage, on their part, the study of contraception in its practical aspects, to impede the com-

parison of thoughts and new ideas, and to check the
interest in inventions and discoveries which the people
at large are in need of.  Of this subject everyone has
that little knowledge which is a dangerous thing.  The
mass of the people believe in contraception, and practice
those arts with which they are familiar, often knowing
them to be objectionable on some account, often fearing
that the methods known to them may be physically injurious, and ever looking to the medical profession for
advice to guide them in better and safer methods; but
among physicians themselves there is a vast amount of
ignorance on the subject, and comparatively few are well
enough informed about it to give such advice as is
naturally expected of them.  Many physicians are, like
all other classes, seeking information, and are anxious
to compare notes and experiences, but with the channels
of interchange blockaded, each has to observe and learn
for himself.  They hesitate to take the responsibility of
advising, and so their consultants turn to their own
resources, and follow one method and another until they
discover for themselves the evil or injurious results.
Thus it happens that probably more than one-half the
adult population of the United States are resorting to
practices which have been truly called

### "Conjugal Sins."

Sins, the nature and result of which they should be
instructed about according to the best and latest light of
sexual physiology.  For the lack of such instruction
they go on sinning against laws of health and nature
which are inexorable, and whose penalties cannot be
escaped through any scheme of vicarious atonement.
For the purpose of this argument there is no need of
specifying or listing the conjugal sins referred to, but it
may be said that the neglect on the part of physicians to

THE RADICAL REMEDY IN SOCIAL SCIENCE.

take a hand in the discussion of this subject, has led to the handling of it in a rather unfortunate way by persons of excellent motives, but lacking the requisite knowledge or experience of physiology and disease to enable them to advise wisely and well. The pamphlets issued in the interests of the Neo-Malthusian propaganda, in England, have, in the main, been the work of such persons, and have doubtless created, to a large extent, an opinion more favorable to the harmlessness of several well known methods of contraception than would be accorded them by physicians who have studied the question from all sides. This remark applies especially to the custom said to be so prevalent among the French Peasantry, the plan which Dr. Routh so severely denounced, and to the use of strong injections of cheap and crude chemicals, which, as a common resource, must surely produce evil results upon mucous membranes. In spite of the fact that physicians' hands are tied by the laws here criticized, many minds in the profession have been hard at work on these problems, but the serious fact is that they have, as a rule, been so intimidated that the world has not been able to profit by their work. There is a great deal of strong sentiment against the laws among physicians, and if a secret vote could be had on the proposition to repeal them, they would have to go by a large majority of the popular vote; but one, and perhaps the great reason why there is no great effort of this kind is, as I have remarked and as I will again have reason to show farther on, because the laws are as little enforced as are the Sunday liquor laws; and like all prohibitory laws, they are mainly disregarded by those persons who evade them not on principle, but for revenue only, and the class or quality of articles furnished is, as a rule, objectionable, spurious or even dangerous. Nevertheless the popular demand is so freely supplied that few complaints are heard from

the masses, and the objections are made by those who
dare defend a principle and urge reform.

### Contraception Among the "Crooks" Should be Facilitated by the State.

We have referred above to a third class of persons who
might be affected by the enforcement of laws against
contraceptics, the criminal, vagrant and pauper classes,
but it would be difficult to show that they are in any way
inconvenienced thereby, for they are in everything so
reckless and irresponsible that it is doubtful if they can
be fairly included among the patrons of contraceptic
arts.    We were reminded of them by the testimony given
at the recent court trial already referred to in this
chapter, in which the informer alluded to "crooked
women" as customers for the goods he was purchasing
at wholesale.    It then occurred that we wondered
whether it were possible that anyone would consider it
good public policy to put such things out of the reach of
that class *et hoc genus omne*.  Shall the State favor the
breeding of harlots, criminals and their ilk, by with-
holding from them the means of restraining their
fecundity?  Fortunately their irregular, unnatural habits
of living, and their proneness to diseases which themselves contracept and cause sterility, do a great deal to
limit their increase, and when the State awakens to
wisdom, it will do what it can to assist in restraining the
fertility of these classes.    More rash prophecies have
been made than this: THAT SOMETIME THE STATE WILL
DEEM IT EXPEDIENT TO DISTRIBUTE CONTRACEPTICS AMONG
THOSE TOO NEGLIGENT TO OBTAIN THEM AS FREELY AS IT NOW
SUPPLIES VACCINATION.    It might be claimed that this plan
has already been adopted in England, for, as Mrs. Annie
Besant shows in "The Law of Population," it is the
custom for physicians of the hospitals for contagious
diseases, in dismissing the women, to "instruct them to

keep themselves clean, to use injections and lotions." Mrs. Besant remarks, "these women are not meant to bear children; they are to be kept 'fit for use' by Her Majesty's soldiers." The fact that one girl raised in an almshouse in the State of New York, and going thence to lead a disolute life, contributed to the population in her descendants, 200 criminals, 280 paupers and 50 prostitutes, whose parentage it was possible to trace back to her, shows what might have been saved the State had that woman gone forth from its charge provided with the sense, the knowledge and the means to protect herself, as she would probably have been glad to do, against the exuberance of her own fertility. Ten cents worth of lock for that pandora's box might have saved a million and a quarter of dollars to the public purse, which is known to have been the expense of pursuing the evils that escaped from it. This suggestion is not offered without a consciousness of its novelty, and of the extreme liability that it will be met by strong prejudices, but that any valid reasons can be cited against its utility we shall be slow to believe.

### Suppression Practically Impossible.

The fourth class of persons who might be affected by the anti-contraceptic legislation includes those young unmarried persons whose virtue is of such thin veneer that it will not stand the wear of opportunity nor the tear of temptation without the full fear of consequences. Mrs. Besant's reply to this charge, already quoted, is sufficient, so far as it goes, but the point which has been too often overlooked is the impossibility of affording to this sickly sort of virtue the protection which it is the main object of the law to provide. It simply is not possible to withhold, suppress or destroy all the expedients of common resort as contraceptics, and will not be until the dial of science and progress shall have turned back a thousand years, when all physiological books may be consigned to flames, and the dark shroud of ignorance be allowed to settle down over all as completely as in the tenth century; not until even the Bible * itself shall have been taken out of the possession of the masses, and relegated to the care of monasteries.

As for articles themselves it will not be possible to suppress them while there remains a legitimate use for such things as syringes,† sponges, cotton, pessaries‡ and vaseline, and as for scientific facts in any department of knowledge, the whole spirit of the age and the nation is in favor of broadest possible education, at the same time holding all responsible for the use they make of their education. No one is silly enough to propose that instruction in penmanship be done away with because experts in the art have so often made use of it for

---

* While people are permitted and advised to study the scriptures diligently, and while the passage remains relating how Onan evaded the responsibility which devolved upon him under Hebrew law to "raise up seed to thy brother," (Genesis, xxxviii , 9), it is evidently impossible to conceal the first recorded, the best known and, unfortunately, from the hygienist's point of view, one of the most objectionable methods of contraception.

† In the trial of E. H. Heywood in the U. S. Court of Boston, April 10th, 1883, Judge T. L. Nelson, in his charge to the jury, said: "The Government must prove that the article advertised is an article designed or intended for the prevention of conception. That is a material allegation in the indictment; that is a question for your consideration. The defendant has put into the case an article which is called the Comstock syringe. Now, whatever the words of the advertisement may mean, unless the article advertised is designed or intended for this particular purpose, the charge has not been proved." No such proof was offered and the defendant was acquitted. It would seem that under such ruling almost every syringe prosecution must fail, for they all have, and are presumably designed for legitimate purposes, though they may be applied by "designing" persons to the purpose which the law prescribes as unlawful. This proves the impracticability of suppressing this large and available class of contraceptics.

‡ In a trial at the Court of General Sessions, New York, March 8th, 1886, Judge Cowing presiding, important points were decided in reference to closed-ring-pessaries, as brought out by the testimony and the Judge's charge to the jury. Expert testimony

forgery; and though dynamite is more widely known
and understood in its abuse than in its use, no one has
yet shown himself foolish or bigoted enough to propose
that all books describing how to manufacture and handle
it should be proscribed.   In the progress of science and
art there are innumerable discoveries which can be
turned to good or evil use, and the only practical protection against the latter is to hold the offender responsible who employs a good thing for an evil purpose.

### Chastity that is Worth Preserving.

Robert Dale Owen has said some good and true things,
bearing on this discussion, in his "Moral Physiology:"
"That chastity which is worth preserving is not the
chastity that owes its birth to fear and ignorance.
*   *   *   The virtue of ignorance is a sickly plant, ever

---

showed that these articles served useful and legitimate purposes
in the treatment of uterine diseases, but the prosecution produced
evidence to show that the defendant in this case had sold them
with a circular making known their utility as contraceptics.  The
following is part of the Judge's charge, phonographically reported :
"Courts of justice have nothing to do with the propriety of the
laws.  Courts of justice are instituted for the purpose of enforcing
laws, and for that alone.  You are part of the court, and it is your
duty to assist the court in administering the laws as we find them.
Whether they are good and expedient does not come up before us
at all.  As to whether this law which forbids the sale of articles
for prevention of conception is expedient, you have nothing to do.
We are not called upon to philosophize as to whether it is wise or
unwise, but we find it on the statute books, and it is our duty to
administer it. * * *  If this defendant sold this gross of womb-veils
for a lawful purpose, even though they could be used for an unlawful purpose, he is not guilty ; but if he for an unlawful purpose
sold these veils, to wit, for the prevention of conception, then he
is guilty.  That is the issue which you are called upon to determine. *  *  *  If his purpose was lawful, I should acquit him at
once.  If it was for having them used for prevention of conception,
he has violated the law, and ought to expect to take the consequences. *  *  *  If you take the view of this case which the defendant claims, that those articles were manufactured for a lawful
purpose, that they were sold, if at all, with the red circular"
(describing them as womb-supporters and medicine appliers), "it
goes without saying that this defendant should be acquitted."

exposed to the caterpillar of corruption, liable to be scorched and blasted even by the free light of heaven; of precarious growth; and, if at last artificially matured, of little or no real value.  *  *  *  In the monkish days of mental darkness, when it was taught and believed, that all the imaginations and all the thoughts of men are only evil continually -when it was deemed right and proper to secure the submission of the masses by with-holding from them the knowledge even how to read and write- in those days it was all very well to shut up the physiological page, and tell us, on the day we read therein we shall surely die.  But those times are past. In this nineteenth century men and women read, think, discuss, inquire and judge for themselves.  If, in these later days there is to be virtue at all, she must be the offspring of knowledge and free inquiry, not of ignor-ance and mystery.  We *cannot* prevent the spread of any real knowledge, even if we would; we *ought* not, even if we could."

Certain it is that a very large amount of knowledge as to the physiology of conception and the means of pre-vention is already abroad among the people, and the general complaint is not a lack of knowing some way, but a desire to know which way is least objectionable. Neither is ignorance bliss for young women, in sexual physiology, as some stoutly maintain, for physicians are constantly having piteous appeals from those unfortu-nate ones whose mental ignorance and trusting disposi-tion has led to serious complications, and when a physician is brought face to face with a young unmar-ried woman whom he finds to be enciente *without knowing what it means* when he informs her, he naturally loses regard for "innocence" and concludes that there is an amount of ignorance which is not bliss—that there is a folly in wisdom worthy of commendation.

## Retrospect.

In stating the objections to the Alphite theory of sex ethics, showing that it is not a practical working formula for the people of this day and generation, and that it is not even proven to be the last, best and only solution of the problem in accord with the nature of things and with a sound philosophy of life; and in demonstrating that the policy of the second party is unnecessarily "limited," narrow, illogical and impolitic, and that what they aim to accomplish is, from the nature of the case, impractica- ble, that to the extent their restrictive aims achieve any- thing, the result is unfair, unequal, and tends to en- courage worse vices than those they suppress, and that if prohibition were practical, it could only be so by an abrogation of personal rights and liberties, and by a gross interference with strictly private family affairs; in these arguments enough has been said to show that the only sensible, logical, and, from a constitutional stand- point, tenable ground, is that of the third party, or "those who believe that the science and art of contra- ception should be studied, developed and improved, and that what is known or hereafter to be discovered should be published, as is all science, without fear or favor."

Offering the above with a firm conviction in its irre- futable verity, we append the just reasons of our oppo- sition to the present status of the laws of New York State, and several other states, as well as the Comstock postal law. We protest:

1st. That abortion is accorded a legitimate sphere while contraception is not—a provision manifestly impoli- tic, unnatural and immoral.

2nd. That the anti-contraceptic laws are not and cannot be effective in preventing vice (unchastity), because it is simply impossible to enforce them, and even if articles could not be sold in evasive ways, there are methods which no law can reach.

3rd. That if it were possible to enforce them and to suppress all knowledge as to methods, the result would be to discourage early marriage and to favor prostitution.

4th. That their effect thus far has been mainly to interrupt progress and reform in contraceptic arts, and to interfere with those who would make known to the masses the injurious effects of prevalent "conjugal sins."

5th. That they are daily disregarded or evaded by those whose only interest in so doing is for monetary gain, charging exorbitant prices for unreliable, unsatisfactory and hurtful drugs, chemicals or devices, all of which is made easy by the necessary excepting clause of the penal code concerning articles for prevention or treatment of disease.

6th. That all laws not in accord with popular favor, and therefore more honored in the breach than the observance, are a reproach to the government instituting them.

7th. That laws which are permitted for a long term of years to fall into the state of "innocuous desuetude," and then suddenly applied, as these have been, for moral effect, are too convenient engines of malice and not "pro bono publico."

8th. That laws restrictive of citizens' rights or invasive in purely family affairs, are not consistent with democratic government, and ought to be repealed.

9th. That these undemocratic restrictive laws are especially out of place in the United States, in view of the fact that no such laws have been enacted in Great Britain, Germany, France, Holland, Belgium or other continental kingdoms or republics of Europe.

# CHAPTER VI.

## The Voice of the People.

In order to give an idea of the thoughts and feelings of people of all classes, scattered over the United States, this chapter will be made up of letters which we have received during the past ten years (with but one exception, that directed to Mrs. Wilmans), and those which will be quoted are but a small portion of the whole number received. Each may be fairly accepted as a sample of a hundred other almost exactly similar ones which have been destroyed. We preface them with a few words in explanation of how it happens that they were written. In the published works of Dr. Foote, Sr., which have had an enormous circulation, there are several places in which he has advocated forcibly, though briefly, the ideas in reference to contraception, which in this discussion of it have been more elaborated. This has naturally lead persons interested in the subject to write inquiring for further particulars as to practical methods. Owing to adverse laws, it has been necessary to turn away all such inquirers with a printed letter informing them that their paternal parent, Uncle Sam, had undertaken the regulation of their morals, and had practically declared that they must continue to propagate evil as well as good, to sew tares with the wheat, in spite of the fact that his "Human Repair Shops," the hospitals, insane asylums, homes for idiots, imbeciles and defectives, reformatories, prisons and almshouses, were already greatly overcrowded and could not be enlarged fast enough to make room for new-comers. It is no small strain on a sympathetic nature to be obliged to turn the cold shoulder to hundreds of plaintive appeals, like those exhibited in our sample letters, and it is also exasperating to think that some one of them might be a villainous decoy by a hound with the heart of a hyena.

---

[*From Helen Wilmans Woman's World, Chicago, Ill.*]

## An Awful Letter.

My DEAR MRS. WILMANS: I feel that you are the true friend of women, and so I venture to write to you. I don't know that any good can come of it, but it seems as if I must do it just to save myself from insanity. I live on a farm, and we are not able to keep a hired girl. I have five children, the oldest eight years of age, the youngest sixteen months. There would have been one younger but for my own murderous act. I was so weak and miserable and had to work so hard that I just implored my husband to keep me from having another. He is kind to me in the main, but will make no sacrifice for me to keep me from bearing children. When I knew this last one would come I turned wild. Oh! it seemed as if I would rather die a thousand times than go through that awful, awful torture again. I believe my soul did desert me for a time. I left home; I scoured the country on foot and bareheaded for days. At last I tried desperate remedies to kill the unborn child, and succeeded at the risk of my life. But I did not care for my life; I did not care for the thought that my children would be motherless. I had just one desperate desire resting on me like a pall. I could not see one ray of light or hope from under it. There was the eternal round of hard duties; no rest for body or mind. There was the unending sickness that precedes childbirth, and the heavy dragging at back and brain. Life was nothing but an acute consciousness of imposition and cruel wrong. I turned away from thoughts of prayer with a mental curse upon God for making men the lustful creatures they are, and creating women as the tortured receptacles of their lusts.

I want to leave my husband. I am free now. I have killed that last child. I have no more remorse than if I had crushed a worm. I hated my husband so while bearing it that I wanted to murder him. Why I tell you, Mrs. Wilmans, though he is a good man, there has not been a day in five years that I would not have felt it a glorious relief to have him brought home to me dead. He is a reckless horseback rider. Whenever he goes off in the morning on some half-broke colt, my mind will run all day on the prospect of his being brought home dead. And yet he is good, and so fine looking. He has never spoken a cross word to me. Oh! how I could love him, and how proud of him I could be if he only protected me from the result of his lusts. I tell you, Mrs. Wilmans, and I have thought deeply on this subject while dragging about doing my work, that love is one thing and lust another. The man that loves his wife as her heart demands, will protect her from his lusts, and not let them poison her life and ruin her happiness. I have one little girl. When she was born, and they told me it was a girl, I shrieked in terror and dreadful forboding for her. I held her in my arms night after night perfectly sleepless, praying for God to take her. I worshipped the little angel, and this was the best my love could ask for her.

Now, Mrs. Wilmans, I do not want you to hate me. I know I am dreadful wicked, but I am on the verge of suicide or insanity; for I am sure to be in the condition again from which I risked my life to get free, and I cannot stand it. I know other women as bad as I am about this matter. They are good, religious women about everything else; but their religion fails them here. I have talked with a number, and hardly one of them who would not gladly be free from her awful position even if it was the angel of death that set her free.

You heard about that woman who killed her three little girls, but saved the boy. I lived in California then, and was present at her trial. She was going to be confined soon, and oh! such a desperate, hunted-down look as the poor creature had. She confessed to poisoning them, and her only plea was: "They was gals, Judge; don't you understand? They was gals." Only the women in the court-room understood her defense, and it was heartrending to hear them sob and shriek low, kind of under their breath. And the men sat as cool as stones, and judged her and condemned her to death. But the law was saved the expense of strangling its wretched victim, for she died two weeks later in giving birth to a human monster that was buried with her.

Oh, my God! Mrs. Wilmans, how long will we poor wives have to bear so much? Is there no redress for us? Do you know any appliance that will prevent conception? I have heard of such things. If there is anything reliable you will save my life by telling me of it. I've got one of your papers. I read it over and over like the Bible. It seemed as if it revealed a pitying mother God who would take us from under the torture of the father God's cruel law. I know this is blasphemous, but I am desperate; I cannot help it. I will pray for forgiveness when my reprieve comes. I cannot pray now.                                    H. M. L.

### Comments of Mrs. Wilmans of the Woman's World.

"If this dreadful letter had been the first of its kind to reach me, I doubt whether I should have thought seriously of publishing it. But listen while I state a tremendous fact. Nearly every day brings me such letters. As a rule they are not so powerfully written, but they all mean the same thing; namely, race degradation through forced maternity. Women are not permitted under the vile system of inequality that marks the position of the sexes to own their own bodies; not permitted to say when and how often they are willing to bring a child into the world. Thus deprived of all volition in the matter, motherhood from being felt by them to be the blessedest of all boons, has become the curse and terror of the sex. Hence infanticide with its desperate results, and the threatened destruction of the maternal instinct, the noblest and holiest impulse of woman. Marriage under the present reign of the male element is not true marriage in any sense. It is the death of true marriage, and the curse of the race. It is the riveting of the fetters of servitude upon the woman, and the compulsory introduction of thousands of unloved and inferior children into the world. It is the slow but sure slaughter of all the higher and purer faculties and intuitions of women everywhere. It is the murderer of woman's great spiritual nature whose deadly influx converts her into a murderer, and breathes the spirit of murder into the breath of her children. I believe there ought to be a law making it a state prison offence for any man to bring his wife into the desperate condition of this woman whose letter I publish—to actually make a murderer of her. Enforced motherhood should stand on the criminal docket second only to the crime of taking life, and its punishment should be commensurate with its hideousness.

I have written a great deal of woman's financial independence. I have said she would never achieve political liberty until she earned enough money to command the respect which is denied to her in her forced dependence upon man's efforts. But financial independence cannot possibly come to woman, except in isolated cases, where she is forced to spend her whole vitality in the bearing and rearing of children. And I believe now that some appliance for the prevention of conception, that is at the same time harmless and infallible, would do more for the emancipation of women than anything in the world besides.

There is a higher law that would deliver woman from "Under the Curse," but the race is not ripe for it. A few men and women would understand it; a few husbands and wives, who together look with disgust upon our present irrational and animalized marriages, are ready to hear and profit by the spiritual truths on this mighty subject, but they are very few indeed. In nearly every instance where I have sought to inculcate them it has been the casting of pearls before swine. In despair of doing the good I wish to do on this subject, I only feel that I must wait until, through much suffering by women universally, much rebellion against the suffering, and the consequent perplexity and unhappiness of men, both sexes find themselves ready to discard the lust element of marriage, and listen to the doctrine of a pure and ennobling conjugal affection that shall rear only love children in such numbers as may be desired, and that shall lift both husbands and wives above all sin and disease, and confer the boon of unending health, happiness and potency.

Let no one imagine that in the foregoing I have spoken a word against true marriage, the union of one man and one woman on the basis of a mutual love. Such marriages will be the salvation of the race. But, by as much as I revere the true marriage whose cement is love, by so much do I despise that dreadful condition to which most marriages degenerate, in which all attraction of the nobler sort ceases, and each party to the contract becomes to the other simply a selfish necessity for the convenience of the animalized demands of the lower nature."

## A Physician Seeks Advice.

Dr. E. B. Foote, Sr.—*Dear Sir :*

I am a physician, and as such, I write to you for professional counsel as one physician would write to another.

The information which I seek is in relation to my own and my wife's personal health, and *none other.* I believe, and am also borne out in the same belief by other physicians, that my wife has cancer of the stomach. Such being the case, my own professional knowledge concerning her poor health does not justify me in permitting her to have children. She was pregnant some two years ago, but owing to her poor health, she miscarried.

I have often read your work, entitled "Medical Common Sense," which I prize as one of the most valuable works in my library. I should soon be as willing to part with my Gray's, Flint's, Leishman's or any other text book, as to be without it.

Now, as a physician, I can see no reason why professional correspondence cannot be carried on in regard to that as well as any other subject to which professional advice might be asked.

Yours respectfully and fraternally,    D. N. P.

## A Physician Believes in Small Families.

Dr. E. B. Foote—*Dear Sir :*

I am a regular graduate and a registered practising physician. I have read with pleasure some of your writings, and am deeply interested. I am a married man, and have a fine healthy boy with well developed mental and physical qualities. I would ask a favor of you in inquiring the "modus operandi" and construction of safe prudential checks, for I believe firmly that a reasonable number of children can be better cared for and prepared for life's rough battle than can a large family, whose parents are overburdened to even supply them with the necessary wholesome and nourishing food a child so much needs for developing and ripening its physical being. Please find stamp for reply.

Yours respectfully,    C. P. P., M. D.

## A Physician Seeks Information.

Dr. E. B. Foote—*Dear Sir:*

Your circular, also copies of "Health Monthly" at hand. Deeply regret the obstacles you have met in your endeavors to promote the interest of mankind. I have under my care patients to whom your "Words in Pearl for the Married" would have been a great kindness—a great joy—and almost a now life. I was in hopes that I might be able to procure it for them, but would not ask it under existing circumstances. I have great interest in these patients, and would give much to render them the assistance they so much desire—assistance I am not ashamed to confess to you, I cannot render, as this is my first case of the kind, and the older physicians in this section cannot give it to me; will you not kindly assist me with your advice? I can state the case in three words, "too frequent conception." Please let me hear from you.

Very respectfully,        C. B., M.D.

## Hereditary Insanity.

Dr. E. B. Foote—*Dear Sir:*

I have been reading some of your works, "Plain Home Talk" embracing "Medical Common Sense," popular edition, and all I have to regret is that I did not read it sooner, for the reason that my wife has lost her mind since she gave birth to a dear little babe, and is now in the insane asylum. Since she was taken to the asylum, her mother has become insane, and since they have been in this terrible state of health I have been informed that her mother had been in the insane asylum twice before this time. My wife had a slight attack before we were married, and as it seems to be hereditary, and as I was ignorant of this trouble when I married in that family, don't you think it would be better for us to have no more children under the present circumstances? As my wife is seeming well again and will be at home again in a few days, I thought to write to you; and as she has the blessed privilege of coming back to me, will you please send me a prevention to avoid any further increase in family.  Yours truly,  A. L. K.

## Wants to Avoid Propagating Epilepsy.

Dr. E. B. Foote—*Dear Sir:*

I have a copy of your "Hand Book," and find it a perfect little gem. It certainly should find its way into every family. I'll soon order a copy of "Plain Home Talk."

I desire a little information from you—please give it. I have a relative who has epileptic fits, and fears his children (if any should be born) may inherit the same malady. He desires a remedy to prevent his wife's conception.

Be so kind as to let me hear from you at an early day.

Very respectfully yours,        J. H.

## Wants no More Idiots.

Dr. E. B. Foote—*Dear Sir :*

I am like a great many others, will have to ask you for advice, after reading your valuable book of "Common Sense," which has been valuable to me. The fact is, I have made a fatal mistake in marrying my first cousin. We have two children now, and never want any more. The oldest is, or seems to be, a perfect idiot, and the youngest is not much brighter, but I hope that time and age will improve his mental faculty.

My object in writing to you is to obtain your receipt to prevent conception. I honestly ask and crave your sympathy in relieving me of what I consider a sin in bringing offspring into this world of misery. Inclosed you will find ten cents; please send pamphlet entitled "Information for Married People." I hope you will sincerely consider my request and relieve me of my burden.

Yours respectfully,     Mrs. J. M. F.

---

## Insanity Follows Childbirth.

Dr. E. B. Foote—*Dear Sir :*

Imposing confidence in your superior knowledge, I write to ask for information upon the delicate subject of conception, or rather the prevention thereof, by some mechanical means. That I may be fully understood, and that you may see and k now that I am not actuated by any censurable motives, I will give my reason for desiring information on that subject.

In August, 1876, I was married; in July, 1877, our first child was born. Wife did remarkably well for eight days. On the ninth day she became excited and talked vehemently about dying, and manifested strong evidences of insanity, but was never at all violent. She continued so—sometimes worse and sometimes better —for nearly four months, never nursed the babe. After about four months, she became remarkably healthy and cheerful, and continued so until August, 1878, when our second child was born. Wife and babe did well; nursing from the breast, the second child was soon as large as the first. Wife continued in health. March 1, 1881, our third child was born. Everything passed off well until the ninth day, when she became again excited and grew rapidly into a raving, dangerous maniac. I carried her to the insane asylum, April 16, from which place I brought her, October 16, mentally restored. I think she is bloated some. She remembers all occurrences previous to birth of last child, but nothing from just after that until about six weeks before I took her from the asylum. There is no hereditary insanity in the family. The children are all living—the two that I have had to raise without a mother are small but comparatively healthy.

Yours with respect,     C. T. M.

## "Insane Every Time she has a Baby."

DR. E. B. FOOTE—*Dear Sir:*

I send you a few lines again, hoping I may receive some necessary information in my serious trouble. My wife is in the condition that she gets insane every time she has a baby. We have
been married ten years, and we have had six children, of which
four are living. Two years ago she had her fifth baby, when she
got insane the first time. She was taken to the asylum, where she
remained for five months. She came home and was healthy until
she had another; now she is in the asylum since March 17, and
will be there about a month or two yet. This is going rather hard
on us, especially as we are in poor circumstances. I think it is my
duty to quit having any more children. Would you be kind and
tell me of a successful preventive of conception? I need it, and I
got to have it. I enclose a letter from the hospital of November
14, 1880, and one of April 7, 1882. This will prove the truth of my
story. Please answer immediately.

Very respectfully yours, A. B.

## A Methodist "Thinks it About Time to Stop."

DR. E. B. FOOTE—*Dear Sir:*

I am pastor of the M. E. Church at the above-named place. Have
been twice married. Lived with my first wife twelve years, and
have one child, eighteen years of age. My present wife is about
fourteen years younger than myself—my age is forty. We have
four children, all under five years of age. I think it about time to
stop in this line. I write this that you may understand my motive
in writing to you. I enclose ten cents for your pamphlet on "The
Prevention of Conception," and will be glad to have you write me
should you choose to do so on strength of above statements.

Yours truly, * * *

## "For the Sake of my Dear Family."

DR. E. B. FOOTE—*Dear Sir:*

Please accept my thanks for papers sent. I find them very interesting and some valuable information. My wife is of a very weak
condition, and in less than five years has given birth to four children. The attending physician informs us that unless she ceases
to have children, she will not be spared to us much longer. Perhaps you have some other recommendation which surpasses the
one requested; if so, please send sample or paper.

Dear Doctor, for fear you may think I desire them for evil, I will
just say my occupation is a minister, and I would not resort to
anything of the kind, but for the sake of my dear family I make
this request. Doctor, any information or advice will be thankfully
received. Yours truly, J. W. B.

## Application of a Presbyterian Minister.

Dr. E. B. Foote—*Dear Sir:*

I have a copy of " Plain Home Talk," which I have read carefully and much to my edification, and more to my satisfaction,
because it relieved my fears on many subjects.  But to the point.
I am a married man.  My wife is not a delicate woman, but she has
most serious trouble in child-bearing.  She has borne two children,
and in giving birth to each, she came near losing her life.  Particularly was her last labor long and painful with her last child ; so
much so as to necessitate the use of instruments.  The result is
that she has kept her bed for five weeks, and the prospect is that
she will bo there three or four weeks more.  This statement I have
made in view of what I am now going to say, viz.: I do not wish
her to bear any more children.  Now, the question with me is, how
to prevent conception and not do injury to my wife.

This information I am certain you can give, and for this purpose
this letter is written.  I should like to possess your " Words in
Pearl," but I suppose this is not possible.

It may be proper that I tell you I am a minister of the gospel in
the Presbyterian Church.

Yours respectfully,        ·  •  •

## A Minister's Wife "Dragging out a Miserable Existence."

Dr. E. B. Foote—*Dear Sir:*

As I have been a reader of some of your publications for several
years, I thought I would address a few lines to you on a subject of
great interest to me.  I have wanted to write to you for a long
time, but hesitated to do so, not knowing just how to begin, and
now it is like a drowning person grasping at a straw.  In a little
book called " Words in Pearl," you sent me about five years ago,
you spoke of certain modes for the prevention of conception.
You also said it was not worth while for anyone to address you on
the subject, but thinking that perhaps it was different now, I venture to write, as it is something that is on my mind constantly, and
I have determined if there is anything in the bounds of reason that
money will buy, I intend to have it.  Now I do not want to do a
wrong act ; to take or use anything to bring about abortion, but
wish to keep clear of anything of the sort.  I am now the mother
of seven children ; am only thirty-six years old ; just in the prime
of life if I had health, but my health is gone.  I am so nervous I
am not fit to raise my family.  My husband is a minister, and he is
not about the house much of his time, so that family duties fall
heavily on me.  My youngest child is eighteen months old.  I am
in constant dread every day of my life.  I have so much to contend
with when I am in a family way.  I have been afflicted for fifteen
years with female diseases, that almost try my very life.  I have

often thought of writing to you for treatment, but there is so much
to hinder me. I am just dragging out a miserable existence at this
rate, and I write this hoping you will give me some advice as to
what I can do.

My dear Doctor, if you are a friend to suffering humanity, please
answer this favorably, if in your power, and tell me what I can
rely on. I will enclose a stamp for return postage. I have been
in possession of a copy of your book, "Plain Home Talk," for
some time, and like it very much; there is a great deal of good
advice in it. But what I want now is the safest, surest preventive
that can be found, and one that I can rely on at all times, and write
to you in preference to others, feeling sure you can help me out.

Respectfully,          Mrs. * *

## Virtuous for Ten Years; yet They are not Happy.

DR. E. B. FOOTE—*Dear Sir:*

I know a pair of people who have been engaged to be married for
more than ten years, but who, under the circumstances surrounding the case (unless no offspring should be the result of such a
union), feel that it would be wicked to marry, to bring into existence beings who would be physically and mentally weak. I
know from reading your publications, "Plain Home Talk" and
others, that you would regard reproduction, in the case in question, as very wrong, yet what must be done with a love that has
stood the trials and temptations of ten years, growing only more
and more intense with the lapse of time, when there is no reason
under the sun that can be given to justify their continued separa-
tion, except that reproduction would in this case be very unwise?

Being reduced to the last extremity, I have resolved to ask you
a few questions which I am sure will seem very silly to you, but
please be so kind as to answer them immediately, by mail, in a
carefully sealed letter. * * * * *

## Frequent Abortions "Wearing Life Away."

DR. E. B. FOOTE—*Dear Sir:*

I have one of your books, "Plain Home Talk," and since I have
read it, I have concluded to write you. I write to ask if you
will give advice in regard to prevention of conception. I have
been married ten years, and have had one living child eight years
ago. Had one miscarriage before he was born, and have had seven
since; none of them over six months, and four were under three
and a half. The physicians say I will not carry a child full time
again. I feel this trouble is wearing my life away; I want to prevent conception, if possible. My husband and I have consulted
physicians here in regard to the matter, but their remedies have
done me no good.

Very respectfully yours,          Mrs. * * *

## "His Wife is His Comfort."

Dr. E. B. Foote—*Dear Sir:*

Having purchased a copy of your "Plain Home Talk," I ask advice as regards excessive child-bearing. Do I have to answer all those questions or not? I often wish I was barren. I was married ten months when I had my first; it was fifteen months old when the next came, the second thirteen months old when the third came, and so on, until, at the age of thirty-four, I am the mother of seven. My husband will not deny himself in no way except in sickness. I love him dearly, and he is the same: but he says his wife is his comfort. But when I think of the burdens I have to bear, I sometimes feel like being cross to him, but I can't if I try.    Very truly,    Mrs. * *

## "Suffers all but Death" in Childbirth.

Dr. E. B. Foote—*Dear Sir :*

I have, for a long time, been wishing to write and ask your advice upon one of the most delicate of subjects, and have but just found the requisite courage to do so. I beg you to advise me, and I know you will respect the confidence I am about to repose in you. I almost believe you will be able to offer some means of escape from our unpleasant situation. I have been married fifteen years to one of the "best of husbands;" have had eight children, and suffered all but death at the birth of each child. I am very small and fleshy, and four of my children lived but a few hours. I have but two living. I am very nervous, and so are my children. I love them devotedly, and they will be good with no one but mother—no nurse can pacify them at night. My little Frank is twenty-one months old, and since his birth I have not had one night's rest. He is a lovely child, but nervous and restless, and many nights I am walking the floor with him at two and three o'clock, trying to soothe his nervousness, and almost wild myself from loss of sleep and care of baby. He will allow no one else to attend to him nights. Our old doctor says it will kill me to have another child—says I must not. Will you tell me how to prevent it? I am so sorry for my husband; for four years he has known but very little of his wife—and it had been months—and then baby was the consequence. I can be sure of nothing but total abstinence. My sister has so many days when it is safe for her husband, and she strongly urged our trying that way. It proved an unfortunate trial for me, as all known ways do. Can you help us? My husband has only the bonds of marriage, without its rights, for he will not "murder his wife," but I know he feels himself to be unfortunately situated, although he never complains. Whenever I have tried to talk with him, he will say: "Poor child, you cannot help matters, you have enough bear." Let me hear from you as soon as possible. I do feel hopeful in writing to you.
    Yours respectfully,    Mrs. * *

## No Aversion to Children, but Seven Enough.

DR. E. B. FOOTE—*Dear Sir:*

I introduce myself by telling you I am a married woman with a family of nine to work for, seven children, my husband and myself. I once had a good constitution, but it is greatly impaired; my nerves are all unstrung. I have no aversion to children, and think our home would be lonely without them. Our children are all healthy but one; that is scrofulous. I do not believe in crowding children on to a woman until she is all dragged down and does not care for living, and has no energy and thinks her life a failure. My husband is very kind to me when I am sick, and works hard to support his family, but he thinks it is natural for women to have children; God intended they should, and they ought not to complain. I do not believe in abortion or anything of the kind, but if there is anything to prevent a woman from being surrounded with a set of helpless ones, I am for it, provided it is harmless. I am thirty-two years old, and the thoughts of having any more children is anything but pleasant; if I thought there was any sin in preventing such a thing, I would have to try and reconcile myself to my fate; but after reading " Dr. Foote's Plain Home Talk," I think there is a remedy. I feel assured that you can give me the necessary information and remove a burden that cannot otherwise be removed. I implore you to aid me in some way and receive my heartfelt thanks, having all confidence in you that you will not betray my trust, I have confided to you what I would not to a near friend, and hoping to hear from you very soon, I am,

Respectfully yours,        * * *

---

## Two Children and Three Miscarriages in Five Years.

DR. E. B. FOOTE—*Dear Sir:*

I shall endeavor to drop you a few lines to ask you for advice and help, if you will be so kind as to give it to me. Doctor, I wish to confide in you that I may not be betrayed. My life has been an unhappy marriage, and I am compelled to bring in this world a family that will ever be in trouble. Can you not tell me of some means that I may not bring children in this world to suffer? I have not been healthy, as married life does not agree with me. I have had three miscarriages and two children in five years. I find it is killing me. If I could only do something to not have children so often. I have never done anything to cause a miscarriage, with the exception of my last. They come from nothing but grief. Now, Doctor, do tell me you will give me a remedy whereby I may avoid childbearing. I know I could live agreeable with my husband if it were not for the dread of bringing children in this world.

Yours with respect,        * * *

## "Weak and Weary of Life."

DR. E. B. FOOTE—*Dear Sir:*

I bought your book, "Plain Home Talk," as I wanted the receipt what to do not to have any more children, but I do not find it there. I am so sorry; I thought I would write and ask you if you could send me the book or receipt; I can assure you I would never show it to anyone. I am only thirty-eight years old, and have had twelve children. I am so weak that I feel weary of life. If you would answer this for a poor woman, I should feel deeply grateful. My husband only gets one dollar and a half a day, and I feel too poor to have any more children.

Yours respectfully,        Mrs. *

---

## Young, Poor, and Six Children Already.

DR. E. B. FOOTE, SR.—*Dear Sir:*

A few months ago my wife was presented, by a friend, with a copy of your excellent book, entitled "Plain Home Talk and Medical Common Sense," which I have since read with much interest, and I trust, with profit. It has certainly supplied a desideratum long needed by the people at large, as the science of living- so to speak—is presented in plain and intelligent language, suitable to the understanding of the non-professional reader.

The object of this letter is soliciting advice and direction from you on a subject of delicacy, yet one of importance to me and my family, and as you have stated on page 910 of the book, that it is an "invariable" rule with you to answer all inquiries on any subject discussed in that work, I unhesitatingly lay my case before you. It is this: I have been married twelve years last April. As the fruits of the marriage, we have six children; the youngest three months. We are in poor, or at least in moderate circumstances, and any further increase would be hurtful, not only to us and the offspring itself, but to the children already born. It is our heart's wish and desire to raise the children we already have to be useful men and women for themselves and society, but our means are so limited that we cannot hope to give them but a moderate or common school education, and if any more are born to us, we do not see how we can raise them to advantage. We are still young—my wife about thiry and I am thirty-four years—and unless some means are resorted to as a preventive, we may have half a dozen more. Now what we want, you have anticipated. Can you send us a safe and sure remedy for preventing conception? If so, we will be ever thankful, and shall always remember you as a benefactor.

I shall wait anxiously for a reply, which I hope you will soon favor me with.

Yours truly,        * *

## "He will not Stop Procreating."

DR. E. B. FOOTE—*Dear Sir:*

Please send me the pamphlet entitled "A Step Backward." If ever mortal was entitled to a knowledge of anything bearing on a subject of such vital importance to their health and happiness, as I hope this book possesses, it is surely me. Married to one who only looks on a wife as an underling to be used for their pleasure alone; broken down in health from the bearing and rearing of seven children for this man, who then complains of "having so many mouths to feed," taking heart-breaking abuse and even blows from him, I do think I may innocently try to escape similar suffering in the future. We are no more alike physically or mentally than any other extremes can be. My health is so bad that I now only pray to live to raise the children I have already (and who are dearer to me than my own life), but not to be forced to have any more. He has made my daughters, aged thirteen and fifteen years, work out in the field, hoeing in the hot sun, until one became cross-eyed from the strain on her spine, I think, and the oldest one suffers with a constant back and headache. Do you wonder I want no more? And they are growing up in ignorance, too, which hurts me to the heart. Their father is very illiterate, and mainly cares to drudge on a poor old farm, and make his children do the same, at the expense of everything else—health, learning, or the proper housework of women. He says he don't want any more children to feed, but still *he* will not stop the procreating of them; he wants *me* to take something or *do* something to stop having them, however. Please send me the book as soon as possible, and any advice you could give me would be thankfully received.                Yours respectfully,           MRS. * * *

## "The Least Little bit of a Woman"—a Shattered Woman Wants "to get Rested up."

DR. E. B. FOOTE—*Dear Sir:*

Only a short time since I happened to see one of your medical books which belongs to one of my neighbors, and the good and sensible advice therein induced me to address you. You will perceive by this writing that I have no control over my pen whatever; that I am a nervous, shattered woman, and I think that you will think as I do, else I never would have written. I have been married seven years, and have four children, and what I have suffered in becoming the mother of these children, no human tongue can tell. We are not in the best of circumstances, therefore my poor health and raising a large family falls very heavy on my husband, so I come to you for help. Can you—but I need not ask that—will you send me some good way to keep from having children, for a few years at least, until I get rested up? I think I would be healthy if it was not for that. All of my relatives are healthy and strong, but I am the least little bit of a woman, and babies are so large, you know, and I think I have had my share for a while, don't you? Please write and tell me all about it.

Yours respectfully and fraternally,      Mrs.  *  *

## Husband Likes Drink Better Than Wife.

Dr. E. B. Foote—*Dear Sir :*

After perusing your medical work entitled " Plain Home Talk and Medical Common Sense," I write to ask your assistance on a delicate subject, having all confidence in your opinion. First, am married, age twenty-three years, am the mother of two boys, aged respecfully one and three and a half years. Of course this is not such a very large family, but when taken into consideration that I have been obliged to support them with the assistance of my relatives, it is quite large enough. My husband, unfortunately, likes drink better than wife or children, and his wages mainly are spent in pursuits of his own pleasure, and I hope I may never be obliged to have any more children. What I desire is a means of prevention, and I appeal to you, believing you will understand I am not applying for an abortion, but only means of a safe-guard.

Very respectfully yours,      *  *  *

## Continent but not Content.

Dr. E. B. Foote—*Dear Sir :*

I hope you will not be very much bored by another letter from me, but I am in trouble, and some way I feel that you can help me. In the letter I wrote two or three weeks ago, I told you that my husband and I had not dared to live as husband and wife should live for some time, but I did not tell you that it had been six years. At the time that my husband wrote to you, we both realized our condition and knew that we could never live happily the way we were living. He made the effort, then, to obtain help from you, and when that failed, he seemed to think there was no use to try anything else, and that all we could do was to bear our lot with what fortitude we could. We love each other devotedly, and I am absolutely certain that he has always been true to me. He is not unkind, but he has settled into a state of indifference on that subject. It is unnecessary to say that we are both perfectly wretched, and I realize that we can never be otherwise while this state of affairs lasts. You will, perhaps, wonder that I do not consent to have children. You remember I told you that we have one child, six years old, to whom we are both devoted, and you will also remember that I told you that I am delicate. I have had caries of the spine, and since the birth of my child have had falling of the womb. My monthly sickness has always been more or less irregular, though that trouble has yielded to Homœpathic treatment recently. Many of my friends have told me to observe the periods, but our baby was conceived after the tenth day, and I do not think that plan would save me. Others have used mechanical contrivances, but many of them have failed. There surely must be something somewhere for sale that we could use. I feel humiliated that I cannot perform the duties of a wife, and I know that my husband and I will constantly grow farther apart. He is very much absorbed in his business, and I fill my days with social duties, church work and different charities, but our home can never be the happy home it should be until we can live right. I need not say that I have prayed much about this thing, but I know that God helps those who helps themselves, and that is why I write to you. It seems my place to write, too, because I seem to be the one most to blame. No other human being knows anything of this, and our friends think we are very happy. I have hoped always that some way would be shown us, but the trouble grows worse. Surely in your long practice you have discovered some method that you can recommend to us as a certain preventive. If you can help us in this way, I feel sure that you will do so, and you will have our constant gratitude. You will also please inform me what fee you wish. I have trusted you because I know that our unhappy secret is safe with you.

## "Duty Demands"—Law Forbids.

DR. E. B. FOOTE—*Dear Sir:*

Your printed circular and draft returned, is at hand. I fully indorse every word the circular contains, and the laws are not any too strict, but as you say, there are times and circumstances when every honorable physician should use his best judgment and discretion to help their patients out of very serious family troubles. For instance, my case is one of them. I have been married just seven years, and we have our first child living and three dead. The second was still born, the third lived but fourteen days, and showed very great signs of nervousness; the fourth was still born, although was alive twenty-four hours before it was born. You see that we have had four children in the seven years, and my family physician says that my wife is not able to carry babies through the period. I must insist upon the order being filled. I will not give you away. Bear that in mind. Duty demands that you send the articles. You see by the heading on this paper that I am responsible. Will you confer the favor?

Yours respectfully,       * *

[This editor thinks he is somebody in particular; that the law is good, but may be broken for his special benefit. Such persons don't get even our sympathy.]

## Seduction   Desertion   A Plaintive Appeal.

BUT HOW FORTUNATE, ACCORDING TO COMSTOCK, COLGATE &
CO., THAT THIS SIN WAS NOT COMPOUNDED WITH
THE PREVENTION OF CONCEPTION, AND THAT
HER "SHAME" CANNOT BE CONCEALED.

Dr. E. B. Foote—*Dear Sir:*

During the winter of '80 and '81, I took a course of medicine
with you for chronic catarrh. Last summer I received a letter
from you asking after my health, but neglected to answer it. I
think your treatment entirely cured me of my old trouble, and that,
thanks to your medicines, I have been perfectly healthy for the
past two years.

But I am in serious trouble just now, and as I have the utmost
confidence in you, I come to you for help. Like many another
foolish girl, I have, under promise of marriage, yielded to the
wishes of the man I loved, and now find myself deserted, and unless I can get help from you, with the prospect of, in a few months,
bringing into the world an innocent being to share my disgrace
and shame.

Oh, Dr. Foote, for the love of Heaven, help me! You know how
this disgrace may be averted; help me, and I will bless you to my
dying day. I am the support and comfort of a widowed mother.
This will kill her if she ever knows it; rather than let her know it
I will end my own life, and she must know unless you tell me what
to do; I *will* not live to bear this shame. I never meant to be
wicked—I loved him so—and it is awful for me to bear alone—I
*cannot* and *will not.*

You are a kind-hearted man, I know, and just a few words from
you would help me to rid myself of this trouble and keep the
respect of my friends. For God's sake, don't refuse, I will pay you
anything you wish. I want your book, "Plain Home Talk," but
have forgotten the price. Will you tell me?

Yours in hope,          * *

# CHAPTER VII.

**Barrenness—Sterility, as Induced by Injurious Con-
traceptics.**

Thus far, that is to say, in the preceding chapters of
this pamphlet, attention has been given to the evils,
distresses and complaints arising from too large families, the too frequent repetition of child-bearing, or the
borning of babies under unfavorable conditions ; in
short, the misfortune of having children when for
any reason they are not wanted, and when for that
very reason the unwelcome visitor may be a sad and
blighted child.

We now come to consider the fact that beside the
complaint of "too many" there is the equally unfortunate complaint of "not any." Statistics show that
about one-tenth of married women are without issue,
and our correspondence shows that the state of barrenness is not borne complacently, as a rule, by the wives
who find themselves going year after year without any
prospect of having children. The letters in Chapter
VI could be matched by an equal number of plaintive
appeals from women in great grief because of barrenness—heart sick from hope deferred. Indeed one letter
often brings two complaints, one from a mother overburdened with children, and one from a sister or friend
whose aspirations for motherhood are not gratified;

and husbands, too, are not infrequently heard from on this subject, the ambition for paternity being no less powerful than that for maternity.

In the chapter entitled, "Hints to the Childless" in "Plain Home Talk," it is written: "Barrenness is a word which designates a physical condition abhorrent to every one in married life who has not already become a parent. The idea of being barren is one from which every individual who has been long married, instinctively recoils. With many females the grave is more cheerfully looked forward to than childless longevity, and not a few husbands would rather die in the prime of manhood, leaving an heir, than to live to gray old age and be esteemed incapable of reproduction. The long and short of the matter is that no woman in the secret recesses of her own heart will felicitate herself with the reflection that she is physically incapacitated to bear a child. Aside from the incentive to child-bearing, which proceeds directly from the love of children on the part of woman, the wife naturally fears that she will lose the affections of the husband, if, after many years of marriage there is no issue ; nor is this fear without foundation, for instances are not wanting where separations have occurred simply on this account."

Therefore, in calling attention to the reasons for and importance of regulating reproduction, it may be well, on the other hand, to lay some stress on the statement that the faculty for reproduction must be preserved as well as regulated, and this becomes the more necessary because of the fact that injudicious attempts to control or regulate that function or faculty may actually lead to a temporary or permanent abolition of it. Accepting the statements of competent observers to the effect that early fecundity is apt to retard the full growth and perfect development of women as it will of plants or

animals, that the best and safest period for child-bearing is between twenty and twenty-five years of age,
that the first-born of too young mothers form a large
proportion of weakly or idiotic children, we have
enough physiological reasons to advise the postponement of child-bearing until the twentieth year, even
though marriage be permitted somewhat earlier, and in
special cases there are often individual or family
reasons which make even a further postponement expedient or even necessary.  It almost goes without saying that to effect such postponement it is customary to
resort to various methods of contraception, but it is a
fact equally true, but less well-known or thought of,
that many of the methods which might be called popular, are, through continued use and their own intrinsic
demerits, liable to bring about in the wife a state of
barrenness, sometimes curable, sometimes not.  This
result is almost invariably as much deplored as the
previous condition of easy fecundity was feared, for
whatever may be the reasons at first influential in leading any family to avoid increase, there is pretty sure to
come a time when the reverse sentiment will prevail,
when the family affairs will have been arranged, the
house put in order, the expectations aroused, and
indeed everything made agreeable for the accommoda-
tion of a new member of the family, but if when the
opportunity is offerred he cometh not, then there is
sadness in that household, and may be an exchange of
reproaches.  The husband and wife, lacking any considerable knowledge of sexual physiology, and ignorant
of the possible effects of such crude contraceptic arts
as they have been able to pick up from talks with
married acquaintances, are at a loss to know why children do not come when they are wanted, and are liable
to attribute the infertility to some inherent defect in

the one or the other; whereas, as is certainly true in many instances, the fact is that the practice of contraception by harmful methods has impaired or destroyed the reproductive faculty. This they learn for the first time when they consult a physician as to the cause of their barrenness. It is fortunate for such persons that it is often possible for the physician to suggest a way out of the difficulty, a means of cure of the barrenness when it is merely the result of diseased conditions of the procreative organs that are susceptible of cure, but inasmuch as this condition of what we may call artificial sterility is sometimes irremediable, and since it is always better to avoid such a misfortune than to experience it, though relief be found, we will endeavor to shed some light upon the subject for the benefit of those who desire to understand the reproductive faculty and maintain it unimpaired. Instead of writing a new volume upon sexual physiology, it will be taken for granted that the reader is informed in this line of study at least to the extent made possible by a reading of popular works on the subject, such as "Plain Home Talk," but to refresh the reader's memory, if a little rusty, and to ensure making the exposition plain, a few main facts relating to the process of conception will be restated as occasion requires. Nor will the subject—barrenness—be treated in any exhausive way, as there are many cases of barrenness due to inadaptation of the husband and wife, congenital deformities in either, or to defects caused by accidents, operations or diseases, which need not now be considered. The relation of abortion to barrenness deserves mention here, because of all the methods resorted to for the avoidance of child-bearing it is fair to say that repeated abortion is the most responsible for cases of barrenness. Even one induced abortion may be the cause of a diseased condition of the womb or ovaries which shall make child-bearing ever after an impossibility, or of lesser evils which may with some difficulty be relieved, but repeated abortions, even when not giving rise to any positive serious disease of the generative organs, may induce in them the "abortive habit," so that no product of conception can be successfully carried to full term. It is also worthy of remark that in making a diagnosis of the cause of barrenness, when it is a discoverable diseased condition of certain parts, and in searching for the cause of that condition, it must be remembered that there are many causes which may contribute to the same result, so that in reading what will be said hereafter concerning the conditions of disease so often found as the cause of barrenness, and of the influence of harmful contraceptics in inducing these conditions of disease, the fact is not to be overlooked that other evil influences may have been at work at the same time. Thus, for instance, finding a case in which there is inflammation of the womb and ovaries sufficient to account for barrenness and in which there is a history or long continued reliance upon copious injections of very cold water for contraception, it is not possible to be sure that the latter has been wholly responsible for the former if at the same time the patient has been addicted to tight-lacing and other indiscretions of dress, diet, etc. Or, to put it in another way, the discovery of the existence of any one or more of the diseases which we are about to name as possible results of harmful contraceptics, does not of necessity indicate that they have been the cause, whether they have been used or not; but discovering a condition of disease, whether sufficient to cause barrenness or not, and having the confession of the constant employment of some harmful contraceptic, and not finding any other sufficient cause

for the disease, it is fair in this instance to put the two
together in the relation of cause and effect. In the
consideration of this subject another fact of great importance which must not be forgotten, is that there may
be two apparently identical state of disease, in the one
case with barrenness, and in the other case with average
fecundity; while it is furthermore often a subject of
remark that in one woman a very slight amount of varia-
tion from the normal condition will be attended with
barrenness, while another woman may continue to bear
children pretty regularly in spite of very serious and
exhausting uterine disease. With this preliminary
statement of observations, some of which can be more
easily stated than explained, we will proceed to a more
direct consideration of the use of contraceptics, and
their relation as single or contributing causes to a
variety of diseases of the generative organs.

### CONDITIONS NECESSARY TO PREGNANCY.

Conception, the first step in the process of child-
bearing, requires :

1. A healthy ovary, producing ripening ova, budding
at the surface of the ovary.

2. A clear Fallopian tube, through which the ovum
finds its way to the womb.

3. A womb with healthy lining membrane to afford a
suitable nest for the ovum.

4. A womb with a free cervix, neck or mouth, affording easy access from the vagina.

5. A vagina free from obstructions, unhealthful secretions, or artificial impediments.

6. The deposit of seminal fluids, containing active
sperm cells, near the mouth of womb.

Conception is therefore liable to be prevented by disease of the womb, of the ovaries, of the Fallopian tubes,
of the neck or mouth of the womb, and of the vagina.

Perhaps the most common diseases which cause barrenness are strictured conditions of the neck or cervix of the womb, catarrhal inflammation of the mucous membrane of the womb, (with leucorrhœa), inflammation of the ovaries, and a simple atonic or relaxed and weak state of the womb with lack of suction power, for in the natural state the womb aids in bringing about conception by its own receptive action in taking up the impregnating fluids.

## CONDITIONS UNFAVORABLE TO PREGNANCY.

An inflamed ovary is as unfavorable to conception as an inflamed eye is to good vision ; an inflamed womb is as little fitted for conception as an inflamed stomach is for digestion ; an acrid catarrhal secretion is as hostile to the vitality of the sperm-cell as vinegar. This very minute sperm-cell is in fact a very delicate tissue, and outside of special fluids formed as a vehicle for it, it is like a fish out of water, short-lived. The normally acid secretions of the vagina are not favorable to its long-continued activity. Dr. Simms believes that sperm-cells cannot "live" twelve hours in the vagina, while in the alkaline secretion of the neck of the womb they will remain active two days, according to Dr. Simms, and eight days, as observed by Dr. S. R. Percy. A solution of borax appears to be favorable to their activity, while such fluids as wines, vinegar and solutions of tannic, carbolic and salycilic acids check it ; and lard, vaseline and glycerine are substances of a nature or consistency not inviting to the transport of these migratory cells. Recent observations show that a low temperature does not exert upon them the benumbing effect which has been commonly supposed to result from the direct application of cold. A microscopist who was making some experiments with a view of determining the best way to "mount" them as permanent specimens, tried placing the containing vial upon a block of ice, but in spite of this severe chilling their movements continued very actively during several hours. This of course proves that when cold water injections are employed for their removal the element of cold is not to be considered as efficient, while on the other hand it is objectionable because injurious. The use of cold water injections at a time when the organs are highly suffused with blood is universally condemned by physicians on more than theoretical grounds. Cold water vaginal injections have at best a very narrow range of utility, but their use as indicated is especially to be deprecated. To this cause alone have many physicians felt justified in attributing very obstinate cases of ovaritis (inflammation of the ovary), and uterine catarrhs. Inflammations of the cervix (neck of the womb), thus set up may lead to strictured conditions of that part offering very insurmountable obstruction to pregnancy; or, the depressing effect of the cold thus applied may exert a sort of paralyzing effect upon the womb itself, bringing on the relaxed, atonic state already referred to. This effect is somewhat analogous to the chilling of the stomach with ice water after eating, benumbing its activity, weakening its digestive power, and ultimately setting up a chronic catarrhal inflammation. The use of solutions of sulphate of zinc, alum or carbolic acid, especially when the strength of the solution is carelessly gauged, is objectionable because of the effect which these chemicals have upon mucous membranes, an evil effect in the way of drying, tanning, parching, etc., even to the extent of arousing ulcerative action upon the cervix ; these evil effects being the result of the repeated or too frequent use of such solutions to such membranes, their occasional use in the hands of physicians for the correction of relaxed or catarrhal membranes being their real or legitimate use, so far as they have any. It is suspected that the use of coarse sponges, uncleansed of their spicules and sand, may also have been the cause of such irritable and ulcerous states of the cervix as are often found. There is one especial danger connected with the use of vaginal injections for any purpose, which should be known by every person making use of them, but it applies mainly to the ordinary form of syringe having among its various parts a vaginal pipe. The vaginal pipe, whether of rubber or metal should not have its opening in the end, but rather several small openings about the end. The rectal pipe has but one opening at the end, and if such a pipe be so placed that it enters the mouth of the womb the stream is injected into the body of that organ, and this is a very dangerous thing to do ; even a few drops being enough to produce extreme uterine colic, and fatal p‑ritonitis has followed such a mishap. It might in some cases be possible to introduce the regular vaginal pipe, with side openings, so far into the womb as to make the mistake of injecting a small amount of fluid into it, and therefore it is important in every case that the injecting pipe be carefully kept out of the womb.

## SEXUAL FRAUDULENCY.

The consideration of this subject would not be complete without reference to the rather indistinct relation of Onanism (taking the true scriptural meaning of the word) to sterility. This injurious practice may not be accountable for active or inflammatory disease of the procreative organs, and the recognizable evil effects of it are mainly to be seen in the form of nervous symptoms, but there are cases in which, because of the lack of any considerable local disease or obstructions, it would seem that the persistence of sterility were due to some obscure fault in the nervous mechanism of the womb, a part of the general nervous disturbances brought on by this unwise method of contraception. In woman the relation between the general nervous system and the special nerve distribution of the sexual organs is so intimate that any disease of the latter is almost invariably attended with some form of brain, spine or nerve symptom, and in accord with this evidence of intimate relationship is the frequent observation that what has been called "sexual fraudulency," soon develops in the woman one or more of a varied list of symptoms of serious nervous disorder, such as "nervousness," fretfulness, ˅ headache, backaches, "blues" and chronic melancholia. That sterility should have to be added to this list is not, in view of their profound meaning, surprising.

### WHAT WOMEN SHOULD KNOW.

Dr. Geo. W. Dewey, of Missouri, writes critically of gynecological delusions and deploringly of some fashions of the day or tendencies of the times, in these words : "Our daily papers are filled with cuts and advertisements gynecological (referring to diseases of women). Every reading lady of fifteen is posted on flexures, prolapses and 'female weakness.' A bitter wail comes up from New England that the native population are becoming extinct. Syringes, sponges and womb-veils will exterminate the descendants of the Mayflower. The quidnunctious yankee woman is posted in gynecology. She never breeds. The next decade of aggressive gynecologists will demand a gynecological chair in our female colleges, the business of which will be to teach young women how to avoid conception."

This picture is rather overdrawn, but let us consider its main features, and ask of each "why is this thus." Why are the papers filled with "advertisements gynecological?" Evidently because the great prevalence of diseases of women creates a great demand for means of relief. Why is every lady of fifteen posted on flexures, prolapses and female weakness? Not until lately has it been because she has had an opportunity to read about these conditions, but because she has heard what the doctor has said of the weary invalid women of her own family, her mother, sisters, cousins or her aunts, and the books "For Girls" are good reading for them in informing them how they may escape such suffering. The knowing yankee woman "never breeds"; more truly she "hardly ever breeds." She has seen her mother worn out by overdoing in the line of breeding, and what wonder if she goes to the other extreme! Prof. H. Newell Martin in his college text book upon "The Human Being," writes : "Many a wife who might have led a long and happy life is made an invalid or brought to premature death through being kept in a chronic state of pregnancy. The professor of gynecology in a leading medical school gives it as his deliberate opinion that the majority of American women must at some periods of their lives choose between freedom from pregnancy and early death." The intelligent yankee woman has been as quick to discover this alternative as the eminent professor of gynecology, and she is merely yielding to the common instinct of self-preservation in seeking to protect herself from untimely death by avoiding the chronic state of pregnancy. In so doing she may, indeed she at present probably will, adopt some plan of self-protection which, as has already been explained, is attended with evils peculiar to itself. Therefore we shall hear from the aggressive gynecologist," that women need instruction, *not* how to avoid conception, of which they already have sufficient knowledge to serve this purpose alone, but how to avoid conception without at the same time imperiling their health and inducing a condition of sterility.

### BIRTH MARKED FOR DEATH.

In the autumn of 1886 the daily papers of New York city reported the suicide of a young man eighteen years of age, who had apparently nothing but bright prospects in life, and the only clew to his reason for committing this act of self-destruction was the statement in letters written just before to the effect that he was born to do it.  He wrote to his sister : "I am about realizing a desire that I have entertained to a greater or less extent ever since I began to think of anything.  I know there is something abnormal in my constitution which makes suicide a certainty at some time."  The New York *Tribune* devoted nearly a column of editorial to this case, commenting on the curious state of the man's mind, but offering no explanation of its last queer freak.  To us it seems extremely probable that it was a case of "birth-mark."  His mother, during the time of gestation, may have been in an unwilling mood.  Perhaps she often harbored suicidal thoughts as to herself or fœticidal wishes as to the embryo.  Thus would the child have become marked for self-destruction, and feel that it was born in him that he must take his own life. Thus is illustrated one of the extreme or most serious misfortunes of unwilling motherhood, and there are all grades of lesser evils.  Motherhood may be the highest and holiest sphere of woman, but it is true only of those women who enter this sphere with willing heart and with the intention of consecrating themselves to it as a holy duty.  There is nothing admirable, right or profitable in enforced maternity, and as women awaken to a realization of their own individuality there will be less of it.  Furthermore the time will come when mothers will point with pride only to their achievements, not to their "accidents."

# CHAPTER VIII.

## The Policy of Prevention.

*(From The Health Monthly, May, 1890.)*

AT a meeting of an association of sanitarians held in Worcester, England, as reported by the correspondent of the Medical Record:

"An interesting address was given by Dr. G. Wilson on 'The Policy of Prevention in Some of its Social Aspects,' in which it was pointed out that an immense amount of disease was due to heredity, errors in diet, abuse of luxuries, overwork and worry, and other preventable causes. Dr. Wilson pointed out that, as to the first of these causes—heredity—in addition to the diseased offspring resulting from unhealthy parentage, multitudes of maimed and doomed children resulted from unsuitable or imprudent marriages, apart from diseased parentage. Unthriftiness in marriage too often led to intentional neglect of the children amounting to culpable homicide. It largely accounted for false thrift, under the name of infant life assurance, spreading its baneful influence even into innocent village communities. He doubted whether public opinion was advanced enough to enforce a certificate of health on the part of persons about to marry, but he thought some check should be put upon the appalling waste of infant life by prohibiting marriages unless the man could produce reasonable proof that he was in a position to maintain a wife."

The above quotation is a sample of a sort of writing which it seems to us we see more of now than we did ten years ago, discussing topics which have always been uppermost in our thoughts. THE HEALTH MONTHLY has had a good deal to say upon them ever since its publication was begun, nearly fifteen years

ago.  What seems to be the easiest solution of a certain problem sometimes turns out to be no solution
at all.  The policy of preventing marriage of persons
who cannot give satisfactory assurance of being able
to properly take care of a family has been tried in
some European countries of the monarchal and paternal order, but the laws of men are not infrequently
unable to cope with the laws or forces of nature, and
so it happens that in such countries there is a large
amount of illegitimacy, amounting in some of the
larger cities to nearly half of all the children born.
So the policy of prohibiting marriages does not appear to be a satisfactory check upon reckless propagation.  The more we study these problems, the problem how to bring about a better average of viable
children, how to save the waste to the family and the
nation involved in the bringing forth of weak specimens, doomed to early death, the problem of saving
unnecessary wear and tear upon mothers, of saving
to fathers the impoverishing expenses attending the
birth and death of such children, the problem in general of how to born better babies and of raising a
new generation that shall be a credit and service to
the community—the more we get riveted to the notion
that it can only be by educating the fathers and
mothers of to-day, and especially young persons about
to form new family ties, in the facts and science of
hygiene and heredity so far as they are already known,
and in the art of regulating reproduction by controlling conception.

This is a matter which we have already considered
at length in our pamphlet, entitled "Borning Better
Babies" which is now probably in the possession of a
large number of our readers.  But such articles as
the one above quoted and some letters from which we

are about to quote tempt us to the writing of this article, reviewing the subject.

### Extracts from Late Letters.

A scolding correspondent asks: "What in creation do you write such books for? You tell us we should not have more children than we can take care of, but you do not tell us how we can keep from having them. If you won't tell us, what is the use of writing all that stuff anyway? I have had two babies and one miscarriage in less than three years. I know my health will soon be gone if it goes on in this way much longer. I have a good, kind husband whom I love and who loves me, but we don't want any more children right away at least." This lady is evidently in dead earnest. She is disgusted and doesn't hesitate to say so, because we do not boldly defy the law, and give her the information she desires, and which we are free to admit she has a right to have. We need but mention briefly that the United States postal law prohibits us from writing the book, or adding to books already written the chapter which she is so anxious for. It is, of course, a constant source of irritation to us that we cannot aid as we would like correspondents of this class.

Here is another from a young man who wants the same information because he is anxious to marry but cannot afford to do so if paternity must be a sequence. He says: "It is not because I do not desire to have children. I am a man of strong affections and would like nothing better than to have a home with wife and children surrounding me. I would like to be married on account of the temptations that beset a young man," etc. We have a companion letter from a young woman, living with a stepmother, who is ready to marry a poor, young man, being anxious to live in happier relations, but they do not feel that they can take that step without being insured against the too early event of children.

### Poor Stock to Breed From.

Here is another letter from the unfortunate wife of a brutal, drunken man. She already has one child with St. Vitus' dance, and wants to save herself from having more sickly or possibly weak-minded children by such a father. As a companion to this we have a letter from a woman in Detroit whose husband has been under treatment in an insane asylum, insanity being hereditary in his family. She already has three children by him, but makes no comment upon their condition. No doubt a knowledge of all the circumstances would lead any humane physician to indorse as correct her desire to avoid having more children.

A lady who writes a very neat hand, says: "When our eldest child was six years and ten days old the fifth was born, a feeble, puny baby, and I am almost broken down. We are devoted to our children but feel it better to regulate their coming into the world so that we can better care for those we have."

Another woman only thirty years of age writes from the frontiers of the wild West that she has been married six years, has four living children, but her health seems to be completely ruined. She fears that she is in the way to have another, and "the idea of it fills my soul with terror. I am so sick and miserable that I am despondent, and I do not know that I am responsible for my actions. How terrible it would be if I should mark my child at such times. We are living in a new country, and have not the means to support a large family. If I could have my health to take care of those that we have, and not have any more at present I think I should be perfectly happy."

We could go on filling page after page of this paper with such recitals and quotations, but these suffice to illustrate the legitimate reasons which many people have for wishing to limit the increase of family. There are certainly conditions where it would be greatly to the advantage of other people too, if such folks could be properly instructed in the means of limitation. Many an overworked and too prolific mother dies from the too great strain put upon her, leaving a large family of orphan children who are likely to fall to the care of relatives or the State. Women's instincts are right and their preferences reasonable in these matters. Most of them desire to have some children, but many naturally shrink from being overburdened.

### Pseudo-Abortives; Demand and Supply.

Now, let us consider what is the result of what we may call State enforced ignorance upon the science and art of preventing conception. In the first place there can be no doubt whatever that it leads to women resorting to the use of such arts as they have come somehow to learn for the production of abortion. Many who would perhaps lift their hands and eyes in horror at the doings of their neighbors, will, when they get into a predicament and in such a frame of mind as indicated in one of the letters above quoted, themselves resort to any means of which they can get a knowledge. It is so easy to find excuses for one's self. Somehow almost every married woman has heard of tansy, pennyroyal and other things called emmenagogues, which are commonly administered in cases of suppressed or delayed menstruation. What-

ever may be the efficacy of such things in mere cases
of delay due to colds or disease, it is doubtful if they
have the power to abort, and yet so prevalent is the
notion that delayed menstruation due to *any cause* can
be brought on by such means we find the newspapers
full of advertisements of "Relief for Ladies" in the
form of "French Lozenges," "Steel and Pennyroyal
Pills," "Compound Tansy Pills," "Cotton-root Pills"
and "Ergot Pills." The circulars of these articles
are so written as not to fall under the ban of the law.
Yet almost any woman, reading that "They are now
taken by thousands of ladies throughout the country
as a preventive of irregularities and as a monthly
regulator, thus relieving those suffering with anguish
and anxiety," would be pretty sure to understand that
the so-called relief or safe remedy "which has been
used by thousands of ladies in America with unvary-
ing success and highly gratifying results in the most
obstinate and prolonged cases of suppression," would
be just the thing to help them out of a condition of
undesired pregnancy.   Unless such a notion prevailed
there would be but small sale for such articles, but
$100,000 a year spent in advertising such things is a
light estimate of the amount thus expended, from
which we can gain some idea of the enormous sale
they must have.   Two letters in our batch, (and by
the way, all herein quoted from have been received
within three months), show how the ordinary woman
is impressed with the advertising of pseudo-abortives,
just described.   One writes, "What are the 'Pennyroyal Pills' so much advertised?   Are they intended
to procure abortion, and will they do it?" while the
other says: "I know you could help me to a preventive if it were not for the good(?) laws of our *free*
country; yet this same country allows 'cotton-root

pills' and other like medicines to be advertised. I am thirty years old, have a house full of little ones, and am so, *so tired.*" If they can do what they are supposed to do what a terrific amount of mal-practice must they be held responsible for. If they cannot do what is expected of them, much injury must they do nevertheless. If the proprietors of any such medicine were to be hauled up in court he would bring plenty of evidence to prove that his pill would not produce miscarriage, but would only act legitimately as an emmenagogue to restore a function delayed by some cause other than pregnancy. So it results that the country can be flooded with circulars and advertisements of articles really sold for the production of abortion, whatever their real effect may be, while it is impossible for a well-meaning physician to give advice in regard to prevention of conception that would be the most effective means of reducing the demand for abortive methods. Physicians well know that rash women after ineffectually and injuriously drugging themselves with these so-called "safe pills" for one or two months, seek out some midwife or specialist in malpractice to accomplish for them what they have failed to do for themselves. In any audience made up of women, of whatever class and reputation for respectability, if one could address them upon this subject and threaten to fling a stone at the head of one who had at some time in her life resorted to miscarriage, it would be as interesting as distressing to see the number of heads that would dodge under. Dr. A. D. L. Napier, writing to the *British Medical Journal* concerning the abuses of pennyroyal for the purpose of inducing early miscarriage, acknowledges that he has been surprised to find how commonly it is thus resorted to and he further says that when this drug or others like it can be successful in bringing on a period which has been naturally suppressed by pregnancy it does so by causing congestion of the womb, leading to a condition of disease which is apt to be distressing and which is likely to render a woman sterile indefinitely.

### Excuses for Resort to Abortion.

Here, for instance, is a letter from a Baptist minister's wife, twenty-eight years old, with six children, who wants to know how to cause abortion at six weeks, and says: "I wish you God speed, so please help me if it lies in your power. I don't want to do any wrong. I am a Baptist minister's wife and a member of the church, but have so many little ones I cannot go to church often." We could match that, too, with a dozen or twenty others if in the last few years we had thought of saving such letters for the purpose. Another recent one comes from a justice of the peace and a high functionary of the Grand Army of the Republic. He says: "My wife is in very delicate health, so much so that the physician that was our family doctor for nine years, said it would be almost sure death for her to have another child and gave us an instrument for producing abortion if she got caught. We have it yet, but deny ourselves rather than use it. I want to know how to prevent conception." It would seem that that family in this degenerate age ought to have almost anything they want as a reward of virtue.

One of the physicians in this city, who stands as high as any, is a professor in a college, and used to teach his class that it was allowable to relieve a woman who could not safely have a child, seventy times seven if necessary, but we never heard a person use severer language in condemnation of prevention than he has used. The *modus operandi* of his reasoning faculties is one of the enigmas we have never had any success in solving.

In a bill to regulate the practice of medicine introduced into the Oregon legislature is a clause revoking licenses for unprofessional conduct, and the first item is, "The procuring, or aiding or abetting in procuring a criminal abortion," and the sixth item is, "Advertising of any medicine or any means whereby the monthly periods of women can be regulated or established *if suppressed*." There were eight items in the list of offenses for which a license may be revoked, but the advising of means for the prevention of conception is not on the list. It is doubtful if that State has any law to interfere with the doctor giving such advice, and yet our eastern States, many of them, put upon the same illegal footing the providing of means for prevention of conception and means for abortion, as though they were equally bad.

### More Education Needed.

What this country needs is a general clearing up of opinions upon these subjects. The morals, customs and health of every family are involved in the understanding of such matters, and, owing to prevalent ignorance, all sorts of evils arise, such as broken-down constitutions, marital infelicity, divorces, cemeteries full of little headstones, and new generations coming up full of the seeds of crime and disease. This is the reason why we write upon these matters often though we cannot furnish the inquirers the information which they feel that they have a right to have from us. We can at least agitate and educate until the limitation of a free press deny this privilege.

The superintendent of city schools in a large western city writes: "I have just read for the fourth or fifth time your "Radical Remedy in Social Science," and firmly believe that no intelligent specimen of the species homo sapiens can read it without becoming a convert to its ideas.  Were it in my power I would place the book in the hands of every adult in the country, and add such practical information as certain shams, known as laws, compel you to withhold."

As to borning bigger babies we have two authorities we wish to quote from, and the first is the inspired utterance of the precocious child whose smart observation is exhibited in this current newspaper squib: "The Way it Struck Her.—A Harlem lady is the mother of a large family of children, and they are all rather diminutive.  A few days after the birth of the youngest a little niece of the lady called to see the baby.  After looking at the tiny specimen a few minutes, the child remarked: 'Aunt Maria, don't you think it would be better to have less of 'em and have 'em bigger.' "

Our second authority is Prof. A. Jacobi, an eminent specialist on diseases of children, who in an article on "Infant Hygiene," thus writes: "It will rest with the social science of the future, controlled by liberality and culture, to determine how far measures shall be taken to prevent child-bearing among women who are immature both in body and years, in order to insure the generation of children with larger frames, and hence better adapted to the conditions of life."

#### How to Favor "Hygienic Organo-Plasty."

Another equally authoritative writer upon hygiene and medicine, Dr. John S. Billings, has this to say: "remembering that the power which we have to mod-

ify plants and animals by regimen and breeding makes
it probable that the human body might in like manner be improved by a sort of hygienic organo-plasty,
to use the phrase of Roger Collard, it might at first
sight appear strange that more attention is not paid
to this branch of preventive medicine; ........ it could
not be done without an amount of interference with
personal freedom which would probably produce evils
much greater than those sought to be avoided, since
to be effectual it would be necessary to work in
accordance with the laws of natural selection, and
prevent the production of weak and unhealthy persons. The little that can be done in this direction
must be effected by parents and teachers." Our con-
tention is that education is needed everywhere, that
parents and teachers, even physicians, need to study
more into the science of reproduction, and that there
should be no "interference with personal freedom"
such as that which now compels a large number of
people to remain in ignorance of the best means of
regulating reproduction, that it is unfortunate that
we must await an indefinite future for that "liberality
and culture" which shall sanction measures to prevent child-bearing among women not fitted for it and
that if there were no State suppression of free speech
on these matters there would be more progress in the
direction of "hygienic organo-plasty" by the people's
own efforts in stirpiculture, impelled by self-interest
and parental pride,—the desire to immortalize themselves by having a few viable, robust children and
giving them the best advantages for perfect development.

As to the "policy of prevention" of the "diseased
offspring resulting from unhealthy parentage" by attempt of State to limit, prevent or regulate marriage

and parentage, we have no good opinion of its propriety or practicability, and as to "the policy of prevention" by State laws of publication of best ways and means for limitation of family increase, we consider it an abominable interference with personal freedom which produces evils greater than those thereby avoided ; and just because so many who think as we do are too mealy-mouthed to stand forth and protest against such legislation, we are persistent in our arguments against it, hoping that thereby we may some day be able to show "what is the use of writing all that stuff anyway."

# WORDS FOR LIBERTY.

" For always in thine eyes, O Liberty !
Shines that high light whereby the world is saved ;
And though thou slay us, we will trust in thee."
*—John Hay.*

"Give me liberty to know, to utter, and to argue freely, according
to conscience, above all liberties."*—Milton.*

"Congress shall make no law respecting an establishment of
religion, or prohibiting the free exercise thereof ; or abridging the
freedom of speech, or of the press ; or the right of people peaceably
to assemble, and to petition the Government for redress of griev-
ances."*—Art. 1, of the Amendments to the U. S. Constitution.*

"Whoso would be a man, must be a non-conformist. He who
would gather immortal palms must not be hindered by the name
of goodness, but must explore if it be goodness. Nothing is at last
sacred save the integrity of your own mind."*—Emerson.*

"All silencing of discussion is assumption of infallibility. If
all mankind, minus one, were of one opinion, and only one person
were of the contrary opinion, mankind would be no more justified
in silencing that one person than he, if he had the power, would
be justified in silencing mankind."*—John Stuart Mill, Essay on
Liberty.*

"To the pure all things are pure, not only meats and drinks, but
all kinds of knowledge, whether of good or evil ; the knowledge
cannot defile, nor consequently the books, if the will and conscience be not defiled. Whereof what better witness can ye expect
I should produce, then one of your own now sitting in Parliament,
the chief of learned men reputed in this land, Mr. Selden, whose
volume of natural and national laws proves, not only by great
authorities brought together, but by exquisite reasons and
theorems almost mathematically demonstrative, that all opinions,
yea errors, known, read and collated, are of main service and
assistance towards the speedy attainment of what is truest."*—
Milton's " Areopagitica."*

"To suffer the Civil Magistrate to intrude his powers into the
field of opinion and to restrain the profession or propagation of
principles on the supposition of their ill tendency, is a dangerous
fallacy which at once destroys all religious liberty ; it is time
enough for the rightful purposes of Civil Government for its officers to interfere when principles break out into overt acts against
peace and good order."*—Thomas Jefferson, in the Virginia House
of Delegates in* 1785.

"It is proper to take alarm at the first experiment on our
liberties. We hold this prudent jealousy to be the first duty of
citizens and one of the noblest characteristics of the late revolu-
tion. The freemen of America did not wait until usurped power

had strengthened itself by exercise and entangled the question in precincts. They saw all the consequences in the principle, and they avoided the consequences by denying the principle. We revere this lesson too much to forget it."—*Madison.*

"You retain the forms of freedom, but so far as I can gather there has been considerable loss of the substance. Free institutions can only be maintained by citizens, each of whom is instant to oppose every illegitimate act, every assumption of supremacy, every official excess of power, however trivial it may seem. As Hamlet says, there is such a thing as 'Greatly to find quarrel in a straw,' when the straw implies a principle. * * * As one of your earlier statesmen said: 'The price of liberty is eternal vigilance.' But it is far less against foreign aggressions upon national liberty that this vigilance is required, than against the insidious growth of domestic interferences with personal liberty."—*Herbert Spencer.*

"Once let it be admitted that the publication of any book or pamphlet is in good faith, meant for public good, entirely free from corrupt motives, and it cannot be suppressed without violation of the fundamental principles of liberty. This would appear at once if such suppression were equitably applied to all works which are liable to the charge of offending the conventional moral sentiment. Goethe, being once in Kiel, was invited to attend a meeting called by some clergymen for the suppression of obscene literature. He attended, and proposed that they should begin with the Bible. That ended the conference, and it was never heard of again; and that will end all these attempts to suppress books called immoral by prurient imaginations just as soon as the same measure is meted out to freethinkers and Bible societies."—*M. D. Conway.*

"The great principles of American liberty are still the lawful inheritance of the people, and ever should be. The right of trial by jury, the habeas corpus, the liberty of the press, the freedom of speech, the natural rights of persons, and the rights of property must be preserved. * * * The entire freedom of thought and speech, however acrimoniously indulged, is consistent with the noblest aspirations of man and the happiest conditions of the race. The maxims that in all intellectual contests truth is mighty and must prevail, and that error is harmless when reason is left to combat it, are not only sound but salutary, it is a poor compliment to the merits of a cause that its advocates would silence opposition by force; and generally those only who are in the wrong will resort to this ungenerous measure."—*General Hancock.*

"Nor can any regulation be enforced against the transport of printed matter in the mail which is open to examination, so as to interfere in any manner with the freedom of the press, or with any rights of the people. Liberty of circulating is as essential to that freedom as liberty of publishing; indeed, without the liberty of circulation the liberty of publication would be of little value."—*Chief Justice Field, June 4, 1878.*

## A CURIOUS SAVAGE CUSTOM.

HOW THE "BLACKS," ABORIGINEES OF AUSTRALIA
HAVE SOLVED THE POPULATION PROBLEM TO
THIER SATISFACTION.

"Among Cannibals," by Carl Lumholtz, published
by Charles Scribner's Sons, 1889, has this on page 47:

"During my sojourn here (Western Queensland,
Australia) I had the good luck to obtain a valuable
flint knife which the natives of the Georgina river
use for the peculiar mica operation to prevent the
increase of population. It has a very sharp point
and three sides, two of which are very sharp, so that
the blade is in fact two-edged. This flint knife is the
finest Australian implement I have seen. One would
hardly think it was made by an Australian native, so
much labor has been bestowed upon it." A foot-note
says:

"This remarkable custom, by which the natives
produce hypospadi artificially, belongs especially to
the tribes west of the Diamantina river, and west
and north of the Gulf of Carpentaria, and does not,
as might be supposed, originate in lack of means of
sustenance, since the districts in question are full of
rats, fish, and such vegetables as nardu, pig weed
and the like. In a few tribes the children are operated on, only about five per cent. being spared. In
other tribes it is the husband who, after becoming
the father of one or two children, must submit to the
requirements of the law, as it is said, amid certain
festivities (as for example trees are cut down and

stuck into the ground in a circle about the place of the operation).   A man about twenty years old from the Georgina river whom I examined, explained to me that the reason for the operation was, that the blacks "did not like to hear children cry in the camp," and that they do not care to have many children.   This person had not been operated on himself, as he had not yet been the father of a child.   According to the information I gathered, the cut, which is about an inch long, extends almost to the scrotum (behind it).   The surface of the wound is burnt with hot stones, whereupon the wound is kept apart by little sticks which are inserted, and in this manner an opening is formed through which the sperm is emitted.   The natives of these tribes are fat, and in good physical condition.   Mr. White, a squatter from Rocklands in Nortwestern Queensland, and an excellent observer of the blacks, noticed for the first time in 1876, near Boula, that some of them had been injured in some way, and found that they had been operated on in the manner described.   Later, he saw a number of cases, and they all explained to him that the reason was that they did not care to be burdened with too many children.   (See in regard to this custom also two articles by Baron N. Von Miclucho-Maclay in Zeitschrift fur Ethnologie.   Berlin, 1880 and 1882.)

On page 44 Lumholtz says: "The natives near Diamantina river astonished me by their bodily structure; neither before nor since have I seen them so tall and upon the whole so well nourished as in the tribe near Elderslie.   Some of the women were even monstrously large; their hair was generally straight.   Their food consisted mainly of fish, snakes, rats and claims."

# Bibliography.

"Essay on the Principle of Population;" by T. R. Malthus, London, 1798, 1803, 1807, 1817, 1826. Reprinted of late by Reeves & Turner, London.

"Malthus and His Works;" by James Bonar, M.D. Harper's Handy Series, No. 28.

"Principles of Political Economy;" by J. S. Mill, London, 1876. Little, Brown & Co., of Boston.

"Elements of Social Science; An Exposition of the True Cause and Only Cure of the Three Primary Social Evils: Poverty, Prostitution, Celibacy;" by a Doctor of Medicine, London, 1854—1877. Edward Truelove, 256 High Holborn. Price three shillings.

"Illustrations and Proofs of the Principle of Population;" by Francis Place, London, 1822. Longman, Hurst & Brown.

"Every Woman's Book;" by Richard Carlisle, London. (Out of print).

"Moral Physiology;" by Robert Dale Owen, New York, 1830, G. Vale. Boston, 1875, J. P. Mendum.

"Fruits of Philosophy;" by Charles Knowlton, M.D. Boston, 1833. London, 1877, Freethought Publishing Co.

"The Population Question;" by C. R. Drysdale, M.D., London. Malthusian League, 63 Fleet street, E. C. Price six pence.

"Poverty; Its Cause and Cure;" by M. G. H., London. E. Truelove, 256 High Holborn (1884). Price one penny.

"Early Marriage and Late Parentage; the Only Solution of the Social Problem;" by Oxoniensis, London. George Standring, 8 Finsbury street, E. C. Price three pence.

"Du Principe de Population;" par Joseph Garnier, Paris. Garnier Freres, Rue Des Saints Peres, 6. Price fifteen francs.

"De Voorhehoedmiddelen Tegen Zwangerschap;" door J. Schoondermark, Jr. Amsterdam, A. Von Klaveren.

"Der Malthusianismus in Sittlicher Beziehung;" von Hans Ferdy, Berlin. Louis Heuser's Verlag. Price one mark.

"The Wife's Handbook;" by Dr. H. A. Allbutt, M.R. C.P.E., etc., Leeds, England. (Announced).

"The Malthusian;" Monthly Journal; Organ of the Malthusian League, London. 63 Fleet street, E.C. Subscription, two shillings.

"Scientific Meliorism and the Evolution of Human Happiness;" by Jane Hume Clapperton, London. Kegan Paul, French & Co., 1886. Price $2.

"Plain Home Talk and Medical Common Sense;" by Dr. E. B. Foote, Sr. Murray Hill Publishing Co., 129 East Twenty-eighth street, New York.

# TEN CENT PAMPHLETS.

**OLD EYES** made new without doctors or medicines. How old folks can throw away spectacles.

**CROUP** positively prevented, and cured by means made known in this pamphlet.

**LADIES** learn how to avoid and relieve "diseases of women" by reading Gynecology. Illustrated.

**GRACIE** and Uncle Alex or "pleasures regulated by the laws of health" is a pretty, useful dime novel.

**MARRY** in Haste and Repent at Leisure is poor policy. To choose wisely and love well read Scientific Marriage by Rev. Jesse H. Jones; it tells "how to know one's mate."

**BABY'S** Perils, and Mother's Cares "before, at the time and after," teaches "how to dress baby" in a new way, and what to do for both mother and child during and after labor.

**FOODS** "What's Best to Eat," and "Health Primer, or What the Doctor Says" about daily habits of life, with valuable diet tables for special diseases.

**RUPTURE** cured without surgical operation, by a home-cure method, safe and sure.

**PHIMOSIS** cured without circumcision, by an original plan devised by Dr. Foote, that any man can conveniently carry out himself without pain or harm.

**NERVOUS** debility from "spermatorrhœa" is a pamphlet giving Dr. Foote's ideas of the causes of sexual errors, the results and the means of cure. 10 cts.; 20 cts. sealed.

**VARICOCELE** and other scrotal tumors—telling how to distinguish them, and explaining the relative merits of various methods of treatment.

**FATHERS'** Advice for Boys, about the evils of sexual abuse, by Dr. E. P. Miller; a handy tract ot give to those seeming to need timely words of warning.

**MOTHERS'** Advice to Girls, by Mrs. E. P. Miller. Similar in purpose to the above. 10 cents each.

# MESMERISM---HYPNOTISM.

A Manual of instruction in the history, mysteries, modes of procedure, and arts of mesmerism, clairvoyance, thought reading, etc. Authorized American Reprint of the original Glasgow edition by James Coates' Ph.D., F.A.S., a neat volume in hard board cover, describing the methods of the most celebrated operators.

**How to induce sleep, cultivate psychometry.**
**How to select subjects, and treat them for disease.**
**How to give an entertainment in thought reading.**
**How to fascinate, mesmerize, tame and control animals**

A book full of valuable suggestions, cautiously stated, and evidently prepared by an expert. Price 50 cents.

**MURRAY HILL PUB. CO., 129 E. 28th St., New York.**

www.ingramcontent.com/pod-product-compliance
Lightning Source LLC
Chambersburg PA
CBHW020555270326
41927CB00006B/847